And They Crucified Him

- *Some Thoughts on the Cross*

by
Art Katz

BURNING BUSH PRESS
BEMIDJI, MINNESOTA, USA

AND THEY CRUCIFIED HIM

- Some Thoughts on the Cross

by Art Katz

Copyright © 2011—Art Katz Ministries

These and other materials of a comparable kind can be found at: www.artkatzministries.org

ISBN 10 digit: 0-9825425-2-6
ISBN 13 digit: 978-0-9825425-2-1

Published by Burning Bush Press

First American Edition, 2011

About The Author

Art Katz was born in Brooklyn, New York, of Jewish parents, and raised during the Great Depression and turbulence of World War II. Dropping out of high school, Art became a merchant seaman, and was later drafted into the Army and stationed in post-war Germany. Shattered by the disillusionment and horror of the Holocaust perpetrated against his Jewish kinsmen, Art embraced Marxist and existentialist ideologies as a seeming solution to the vexing human predicament.

Hitchhiking through Europe and the Middle East while on a leave-of-absence from the teaching profession, the cynical and unbelieving atheist, anti-religionist and anti-Christian, was radically apprehended by a God who was actively seeking him. The actual journal of that experience, *Ben Israel – Odyssey of a Modern Jew*, recounts Art's quest for the true meaning to life, which climaxed significantly and symbolically in Jerusalem.

Art attended Santa Monica City College, UCLA, and the University of California at Berkeley, earning Bachelor's and Master's degrees in history, as well as a Master's degree in theology at Luther Seminary, St. Paul, Minnesota. With his speaking ministry as a prophetic voice spanning nearly forty years, Art sought to bring the radical relevance of the Bible's message to contemporary societies, both secular and religious. After a protracted illness, Art passed on to be with the Lord in 2007.

EDITOR'S PREFACE

Art Katz was a prolific speaker, and the contents of this book are comprised exclusively from transcriptions of spoken messages. Published posthumously, and in keeping with Art's desire to have his speakings edited for the reader as well as for literary quality, we have sought to blend approved editing principles with the desire for the reader to "hear" the spirit and voice of the speaker as they read the book.

There are occasions where Art was reading from the writings of another author. Everything has been done to separate out a quote from Art's own thoughts. Any lapse on our part is entirely unintentional. Every effort has been made to identify the source of the material quoted from.

The message of this book may well prove to be Art's most significant and important contribution to the archives of Christian literature. More than anything else, it was Art Katz's deep identification with the cross of crucified Christ that defined his life and ministry. He cherished the "old rugged" cross with a depth of embrace seldom found in contemporary believers.

Art would often say that we needed to examine the meaning of the cross more than any other consideration, more than our yearnings to become sophisticated in understanding the doctrines of the faith, or last days' theology, or any other aspect of our Christian lives. He saw the cross, the crucified Christ, as the "foundation of foundations" without which everything about God and the faith is meaningless. Like the apostle Paul, Art was determined not to know anything but Christ and Him crucified. His knowledge of the reality of God was viewed through the prism of the cross. He saw the logic of the cross as being the basis for defining true reality.

Art insisted that we should continually seek to understand what he called "the pivotal point of the whole faith" until its meaning registered upon us. He lamented how few believers had risen above the prevailing cultural Christianity, or the appropriateness of their correct principles of the faith. He lamented that so few really knew God *as God*. He lamented that so few had "seen God in His greatest act: namely, the revelation of the nature of God in His suffering and death, which has ever and always been His nature." More than in any other place, Art saw that it was the cross that "revealed what God always was and is."

My appreciation to the many who worked on the manuscript. Special thanks to Donna Klindt and Joe Gattuso for providing their remarkable editing skills. Their contributions were invaluable. Thank you to Molly Rogers for her contribution to the proofing process. Many thanks also to Thomas Lei for allowing us to call on his proofing skills. His enthusiasm for facilitating the availability of Art's materials remains steadfast and unwavering.

Simon Hensman
Laporte, Minnesota
August, 2011

AND THEY CRUCIFIED HIM
- *Some Thoughts on the Cross of Christ*

TABLE OF CONTENTS

Introduction…………………………………………... 11

Chapter 1   The Cross and Sin…………………... 15

Chapter 2   The Cross and the Holiness of God… 34

Chapter 3   The Crucifixion of Jesus …………… 44

Chapter 4   The Cross as Suffering…….…........… 52

Chapter 5   The Cross – God Revealed………..... 63

Chapter 6   The Cross and the Triune God …....… 73

Chapter 7   The Cross and Preaching the Gospel... 85

Chapter 8   The Cross and Water Baptism …....… 100

Chapter 9   The Cross as Foolishness ………..… 109

Chapter 10   The Cross and Resurrection……….. 120

Prayer………………………………… 131

INTRODUCTION

In his book, *The Crucified God*, Jürgen Moltmann[1] rightly notes that nothing more sets God forth *as God* than God crucified. We can understand a crucified man, even the Son of God, but the crucified *God* is an astonishing thought. The fact that God, the Creator of all, submitted to a shameful and agonizing death is a profound statement of what His essential nature is.

As much as we celebrate the beneficial aspect of Jesus' sacrificial atonement for the sins of mankind, we need to probe and seek out the remarkable reality *behind* that act. The fact that God chose a point in the history of mankind to set foot in His creation deserves our deepest examination. The fact that He came in the form of a man to make this statement should further arrest our attention. In other words, until we begin to take into our deepest heart the meaning of this event, our Christianity is rendered ineffective—we will be, of all men, most to be pitied. We need, therefore, to have the truth of the crucified God pressed in upon us to bring an ever-fresh appraisal and recognition of its significance.

In the ancient Roman world, death by crucifixion was recognized as the most horrific and shameful death that could be inflicted upon a human soul. The horror of

---

[1] German theologian and Professor Emeritus of Systematic Theology at the University of Tübingen, Germany.

being publicly nailed to a cross lay in its ultimate degradation and humiliating indignity. Why would God choose this form of death for Himself? Why did His Son have to suffer it? What kind of a God is He who would choose crucifixion as being the deepest statement of His nature?

Our understanding of God will be faulty unless we factor in His choice of the cross as the ultimate depiction of His divine being. All that mankind would think appropriate to God's dignity and power is seemingly contradicted by His willingness to suffer a criminal's death. It is almost as if God went out of His way to devastate and contradict every human notion, every man-made image we might have of Him. The scandalous shame of the crucifixion of Jesus demands that our inadequate understanding of God be brought to death. Such a death is needful, for man ever seeks to form his own concept of God. In fact, man *prefers* to fashion God in his own image, appropriate to his self-interest, serving his own purposes and ends. From God's point of view, the cross is calculated to cut through every self-serving disposition in man.

Two thousand years later, the cross is still an offense to the sensibilities of mankind, especially to Jewish mankind. All that the cross represents is calculated by God to contradict everything that man celebrates in his humanity and self-esteem. One's view of man is inextricably joined to one's view of God: one cannot have a view of God independent of one's view of what man is. And it is a spiritual maxim that any view of God that omits what He demonstrated at the cross will never be a true view of God. To see Christ as He is, to contemplate His wounds, to rightly appropriate the reality and truth of the cross brings all that comprises true living into right perspective.

Unless God Himself opens our understanding, the meaning of the cross will continue to elude us. The sad and shallow condition that proliferates in Christendom today is the very evidence that we have not discovered the divine meaning of the cross. For most if not all of us, the revelation of the cross will not come except that we are brought, or allow ourselves to be brought, into a place of darkness, despair and disillusionment. God is waiting for an anguished cry from us in *that* place rather than hearing cheap words *about* our supposed knowledge of the cross. The sooner we acknowledge our falsity, the sooner we can enter into a true understanding of the cross. How many of us are fighting desperately just to avoid that acknowledgement? God yet waits for us to come to an utter destitution of soul where we recognize that our glib phrases about Him stand for nothing. What we say about God might be factually correct and true, but for too many of us it is a knowledge derived from our own inadequate natural reasoning and reading of the scriptures. How many of us misinterpret the circumstances that God brings into our lives to impress that point upon us?

We all carry images of God that are not God as He truly is. God will never force upon us that which is true as long as we are content with the imitation, the lesser thing. He waits for a cry of desperation from us—that He might answer with the true light that only He can give by His Spirit.

Rightly understood, the great truth of the cross will always be a reality that we will never fully comprehend. The cross is *intended* to stretch us. It must and should be ever and always before us, constantly challenging us, constantly deepening our union with God. When the cross becomes something that is fixed, known, a principle that we can refer to easily, then we have lost the cross and its call to the crucified life.

This age is going to end in increasing tumult and perplexity, opposition and tension. The world is dying for the lack of a visible demonstration of the truth and reality of God. There is no more horrible caricature than that the Church should offer it a form of Christianity that is not true, a cross whose meaning we have not adequately apprehended.

CHAPTER 1

The Cross and Sin

Are we sufficiently acquainted with the nature of sin? What, exactly, is this thing that has dogged mankind's steps since the Garden of Eden, this thing we know as sin? Note that we are not asking here what actions constitute sin; we are instead seeking to lay bare the nature of sin itself—its intrinsic essence. We seek here to discover *how* it does what it does. For if we do not know what sin is, then salvation *from* sin will have little meaning for us. Why should we even desire that salvation, and who is this God who saves us?

Most of mankind is devoid of sin-consciousness. Most people are not aware, first of all, that they are sinners by nature—that is, that it is their habit to sin; that to sin is their first inclination, their strongest tendency. We find it hard to acknowledge ourselves as sinners. We would rather consider sin only as a category, a thing apart from who and what we are as humans, a subject of theological discussion rather than an inherent part of the human condition. However, the truth about sin, as well as its consequences, is not found in what *we* think about sin, but rather upon what God tells us about sin and its consequences.

To what then shall we defer: our own human, rational preference, or what God says is the truth of the matter? If we do not have the word of God as the yardstick by which our actions are measured and judged, but give precedence instead to our own assessments, then sin is a very light thing, if it matters at all. However, the statement of God about the human condition is that "there is not a righteous man on earth who continually does good and who never sins."[2] We have an instinctive unwillingness to acknowledge the truth of our condition as God Himself sees and states it. Worse yet, we seem to prefer our own assessment rather than His. Sin has a power that blinds us to its nature and workings; this is what makes sin so deceptive. This answers why we so easily overlook our own sin and call it something else by giving it a more respectable label.

Our view of sin determines how we view and understand God. How can we comprehend God as being holy without knowing *His* attitude toward sin? And if we do not recognize sin, or the evil of it, we will remain victims of its cruel power.

Karl Barth[3] made a point that if it were not for the crucified Christ, the assessment of our own morality and sin would always be favorable. In other words, we will always pronounce a sentence lighter than what is deserved. We will always justify ourselves when we are our own judges. We will make our *own* assessments of our condition. We will rationalize and dismiss the case against ourselves. We will always give a self-flattering, subjective evaluation. As the psalmist says, "Transgression speaks to the ungodly within his heart; there is no fear of God before his eyes. For it flatters him in his own eyes concerning the discovery of his

---

[2] Ecclesiastes 7:20
[3] Swiss theologian from the 20th century

iniquity and the hatred of it."[4]

In His mercy, God does not let us subjectively determine either our own condition or the penalty for it. As we shall see, only the judgment of God upon sin will truly reveal its nature and presence. In other words, we can begin to understand how deceptive sin is by the judgment it incurs. The crucified Christ, therefore, saves us from any self-justifying lightness about our own condition.

There is a Day of God's wrath and reckoning when we will stand before Him and rcccive the consequences and *just* penalty for sin. All of mankind *will* stand before the Judge. The apostle Paul made that clear to his audience in Athens:

> He [God] has fixed a day in which He will judge the world in righteousness through a Man whom He has appointed, having furnished proof to all men by raising Him from the dead.[5]

When the world sees the Judge, it will see a Man with wounds and scars. When it stands before this Judge, who has a complete book that exposes not only its outward conduct but also its secret heart, what then will be its defense?

John Murray[6] writes:

> The essence of sin is to be against God. The person who is against God cannot be right with God, for if we are against God, then God is against us. It could not be otherwise. God cannot be indifferent or complacent toward that which is the contradiction of Himself. His very

---

[4] Psalm 36:1-2
[5] See Acts 17:31
[6] British-born theologian from the 19th century

perfection requires the recoil of righteous indignation and wrath.[7]

Divine wrath is an attribute, an event, a condition, and an action beyond anything we might know as human anger. When God exercises His wrath, He makes a statement about Himself. Would God still be God without His wrath? How does one reconcile His wrath with what He says of Himself as being benevolent, merciful, patient, and kind? What justifies the holy indignation of His wrath when He expresses it as judgment? What is so vile, abhorrent and painful in God's sight and consideration that justifies Him exercising His fierce anger and the penalty of His wrath? Why is sin not as offensive to us as it seems to be to God? These are the great questions that ought to engage our attention.

When David contemplated Bathsheba's naked form before him, God was watching. God knows our secret hearts and inward considerations even before they become an act. Instead of being aware that his thoughts were already known by God, which ought to have embarrassed him, David began to work out those thoughts until the sin itself was consummated. Once consummated, it required further sin: the murder of the woman's husband. Though God had said, "You shall not murder…You shall not commit adultery," David performed those things in His sight, as if God was not present, did not see, and really was not that bothered. Sin has the power to blind us to any consideration of its consequences.

If sin against God is unspeakably vile, then the judgments that came upon David were perfectly just. It is taking liberties as if God does not see, as if He is not

---

[7] Title of book unknown

concerned, as if the act of sinning does not in any way blaspheme[8] Him. The prophet Nathan told David that his conduct had disparaged God and given God's enemies opportunity to blaspheme Him. In other words, God had suffered a loss of honor appropriate to Himself *as God*. When David acknowledged his sin in Psalm 51, he was being churned up in the innermost depth of his soul.

> For I know my transgressions, and my sin is ever before me. Against You, You only, I have sinned and done what is evil in Your sight, so that You are justified when You speak and blameless when You judge.[9]

Note the conjunction between sin and evil. Until we see sin for the evil it is, and that it is *against* God, we do not see as we ought. We will therefore treat sin and its consequences more lightly than it should be addressed, like a man who, perceiving a cobra on a footpath, strides forward nonetheless. Note too that while our sins affect others in many various and damaging ways—affecting many people we could not imagine, in ways that we often do not perceive immediately—every sin is nonetheless always and ultimately a sin against God. Until that reality registers deeply upon our consciousness, we do not rightly understand the true essence of sin.

The judgments that fell upon David were severe:

> Now therefore, the sword shall never depart

---

[8] Webster defines the word as follows: "To speak of or address with impious irreverence; to revile impiously (a sacred thing); as, to *blaspheme* the Holy Spirit." Sinning blasphemes God—that is, it speaks of God's already-pronounced assessment of sin as of little account, as inaccurate, as faulty. In effect, it seeks to make God a liar.

[9] Psalm 51:3-4

from your house, because you have despised Me and have taken the wife of Uriah the Hittite to be your wife.[10]

Though David had committed adultery and murdered a man, God gets to the real issue of the offense: David despised God in his heart. It is one thing to be ignored, mistreated, or slighted, but God uses the word *despised* to describe David's heart toward Him. God equates despising His commandments with despising Himself *as God.* After all that God had given David, he violated God's commandments before His face and in His sight. Is it possible to celebrate God out of one side of our mouth, while, at the same time, despise Him out of the other? Can there be this apparent contradiction in a man whose name means "beloved of God"? David's dishonoring of God reveals the measure of the depravity of *all* mankind. One can indeed go from exalting God to despising Him when the issue of one's lust and gratification is at hand. Yes, it is possible to despise God, though you be a choice psalmist.

> David had despised the Lord and the commandments of the Lord: "Thou shall not kill, Thou shall not commit adultery." But David's actions said, "I *will* commit adultery with Bathsheba and gratify my lust. Despite all that God says, I *will* murder her innocent husband, Uriah, that I might hide my sin and shame by this wicked means, notwithstanding the divine prohibition."[11]

Sin has the power to convince us to act using our own frame of reference rather than God's. It has the

---

[10] 2 Samuel 12:10
[11] From the little-known classic *The Heinousness of Sin* (Author and publisher unknown)

power to convince us that *we* are the final arbiters of right or wrong, that *we* are the final determiners of truth, that *we* are the final Judges. Sin succeeds in convincing us that we are gods of our own little world.

Though God has spoken, how often do we ignore Him and give greater priority to our own desires and reasoning? Perhaps it is because God's integrity and honor are not so immediate or pressing; we do not as easily perceive the integrity and honor of God as we do our own lust and the flesh's pressing needs for gratification. Nor apparently is our desire to uphold God's integrity and honor as strong as our desire to satisfy our own desires. "Against *You* only" was David's deepest lament. Our problem is that we do not deeply know God, the "You" to whom we so casually speak. Though David had a profound knowledge of God, he did not refrain from despising God by despising and disobeying His commandments.

David could say, "My sin is ever before me."[12] Though he was forgiven, he would never forget the sinfulness of his sin. It would haunt him the rest of his life, for he would know that, being once capable of committing so heinous a sin, he would always be capable of doing so again. Sin against God—both thought and action—issues out of our inward constitution of heart. The outworking of sin stems from an ongoing propensity in our life that allows and nurtures it. We are, therefore, responsible for its existence and continuance. In other words, a particular sin is the sum of all the moments that have preceded it rather than a momentary lapse. We all have a history of choices, of indulging in those things that gratify and satisfy us. David did not fully guard his heart with all

---

[12] Psalm 51:3b

diligence in a way that would have honored God. His coming to that place of sinfully despising God reveals a prior history of neglect and indifference towards God.

In the Scriptures, every act of sin is considered an act of rebellion against God. To rebel against His law and authority is to despise God; it is an act of disdain toward His rule and His kingdom. The writer continues:

> A worm of the dust sets himself up above the Most High God, his will above God's, and his interest above God's glory. If God offers heaven, sin despises it. If He threatens hell, sin disregards it. If He pleads the dying love of His Son, the riches of His grace, and beseeches sinners to be reconciled, sin slights it all. He commanded men to do their duty one to another, but sin regards it not. All this notwithstanding His authority over us as His subjects and our obligation to Him as the Lord our God. Thus the Most High is treated with disrespect and contempt.[13]

It would not be so bad if we were taking issue with God from a place of equality, but as *worms*? What are *we* compared to the great Jehovah? How dare we even so much as lift our heads and raise our voices, let alone wickedly perform what is offensive to Him. Sin discredits the honor of God and brings reproach to His great name. If we are really convinced that God is infinitely great and glorious, it will be clear to us that He is infinitely worthy of all of our love, honor, and obedience. To despise and disobey Him is vile. To rise up in rebellion against Him, to act in ways contrary to His will, to treat Him with contempt, is the most wicked thing that can possibly be done. "Against You, You only, I have sinned and done what is evil in Your

---

[13] *The Heinousness of Sin*

sight."[14]

After forty years of guiding Israel through the wilderness, Moses was not permitted entry into the Land of Promise. All he could do was glimpse it from Mount Nebo, but he could not enter. To be denied that entry was a remarkable judgment. The sin that evoked that judgment was the vexation in his spirit whereby he *hit* the rock when he was told to *speak* to it. God was faithful to see that the water flowed out, but God's indictment of Moses was as follows: "You did not treat Me as holy in the midst of the sons of Israel."[15] In other words, "By disobeying My instructions, you misrepresented My character to My people. You are identified as one *with* Me; therefore your conduct is a statement *of* Me, My nature, who I am." In that act of disobedience, Moses neither honored God, nor sanctified Him. He failed to hallow God's name.

God's dealing with Moses is meant to instruct us. If God dealt so severely with Moses, and then chose to be lenient with us, He would contradict Himself. Despite a long relationship in which Moses had been faithful and had borne much for God's name, God could not overlook his sin because His own holiness would have been violated.

Keeping Moses out of the Land would also have cost God much. It was as much an affliction for God who required it as for Moses who suffered it: "In all their affliction He was afflicted."[16] In every judgment pronounced against us, God experiences the moral anguish attendant to those judgments, and yet He does not withhold this aspect of Himself as a righteous Judge.

---

[14] Psalm 51:4a
[15] Deuteronomy 32:51f
[16] Isaiah 63:9a

God is not acting from some lofty height in which He is impervious and unaffected by what He requires of men. His name and character require a judgment appropriate to the sin.

> God is the Creator, we are His creatures and subjects...Do you know that He is your Lord and owner, that He has an entire right to you and an absolute authority over you, that you are entirely dependent upon Him, infinitely indebted to Him, and absolutely under His government? Do you know that the Lord your God is a great God and a great King, infinitely worthy of all love, honor and obedience?

> Do you see what a great evil it is to rise in rebellion against the Most High, to slight His authority, throw off His government, break His laws, go contrary to Him, and do the abominable things which His soul hates? Do you see what contempt this casts upon God, and how it grieves His heart for a worm to set up himself against the Almighty, for a creature absolutely dependent to turn his back upon his Creator, in whose hands are his life and breath?

> Do you see the grievous error of loving sin more than you love an infinitely glorious God, of delighting in earthly pleasure more than in the supreme fountain of all good, of being more concerned to please fellow rebels and secure their favor than to please the sovereign Lord of the universe and secure His favor? Do you see the infinite malignity of such conduct?

> Sinner, if you never saw the great evil of sin, you are to this day a stranger to God and blind to the infinite beauty of His nature. You are under the power of sin and in an impenitent and unpardoned

state.[17]

Perhaps the reason we have not seen God in the measure He can be seen is because our sin obscures our eyes. We are thus blinded to the revelation of His glory and majesty. To the degree that we condescend to sin, we disregard the reality of God as being holy. God is therefore diminished, and we are disposed more and more to find ways of despising and opposing Him.

> Never was a sinner pardoned while impenitent. Never was a sinner truly penitent while insensible of the great evil of sin. Never did a sinner see the great evil before he was first acquainted with the infinitely great and glorious God. If He is no longer great and glorious, or perhaps never was, but is in our image, then the transgressions against Him follow.[18]

If we do not see sin as the abomination and great evil it is, we can never be truly remorseful or repentant. In other words, if we never see the great evil of sin as being sin against God and a despising of Him who is infinitely glorious in Himself, our repentance cannot be genuine. We are living unpardoned lives. That is a hard word for the many thousands who have made a "decision for Christ", or walked down the aisle of a church to "invite Jesus into their heart", in their minds settling in with confidence that they are now "saved", and looking to see what benefits they will now receive. God will say to them that He never knew them, for they never truly saw the great evil of sin.

A wonderful case that makes this truth clear is Paul, who saw himself as the foremost of sinners.[19] When

---

[17] *The Heinousness of Sin*
[18] Ibid.
[19] 1 Timothy 1:15

Paul made this statement, he was referring to his present life as an apostle rather than his pre-Christian life. As he grew in the knowledge of God, and his understanding of God's holiness increased, so too did he grow in the knowledge of his own condition. As we grow in maturity and in the knowledge of God, at the same time there is an increasing consciousness of our inherent disposition to transgress in thought, word, and deed, either by omission or commission. The closer to light, the better we see. We begin to see ourselves as the foremost of sinners; we begin to see ourselves as God sees us. We begin to know what we are capable of, and given the right occasion and temptation, we are just as likely to fall as David.

If sin is feared, we are not going to let our eyes linger a second longer on Bathsheba than the moment accidentally provided. When we allow our eyes to linger, and our thoughts to dwell on what is already evil, we will find ourselves necessarily moving ahead to performing what the thought imagines. Our eyes *will* linger if we do not think that such lingering is evil. We *will* indulge our senses, and finally act in a way to gratify the lust that has been generated by the indulgence. We must never presume that we are too spiritual to fall into sin.

> God can be despised, but the sinner will never feel it or care. His [the sinner's] heart is a heart of stone. If God is abused and injured, an apostate world cares little about it, but if they themselves are wronged, they will highly resent it. They love themselves dearly and deeply.[20]

We are offended when people spurn *us*, but if God is spurned, we barely give it a second thought, thus

---

[20] *The Heinousness of Sin* (Author unknown)

revealing the depth of our self-love. There is nothing that more offends mankind than to be told that, "He who believes in the Son has eternal life; but he who does not obey the Son will not see life, but the wrath of God abides upon him."[21] It is as if God is saying, "What My Son has performed at so excruciating a cost is My great gift to mankind to rescue them from their sin. To reject *that* is to deserve the wrath which abides upon you. The fact that you are not conscious of it, or it is not part of your subjective sense of yourself, does not lessen this truth."

We are called to confront a world that is full of self-righteous assurance, which, if it deigns to acknowledge God, assumes that He is pleased with the way it deports itself. This is a contemptuous disposition toward God, as if *we* can establish the standard that *He* is obliged to honor and respect. We think that if it pleases us, surely it must please Him, but the important thing for *us* is that it pleases *us*. That attitude is sin. If we do not see it now, we will see it in the Day of Judgment when there is no time to remedy our error. If we choose to absent God from our lives now, we will be plunged into an eternity where God is eternally absent. What we sow, we will reap. The writer continues:

> If you do not know the great evil of sin, you know nothing yet as you ought to know. You are a stranger to God, ignorant of your own heart and the deplorable condition you are in. To this day you are unhumbled, impenitent, and unpardoned. Answer these questions and see what is your state. How mournful is the state of Christless sinners who are at enmity with God, rebels against the majesty of heaven. Their frame of heart and

---

[21] John 3:36

manner of life is a continual despising of the Lord, a grief to the holy one of Israel, and a constant provocation.

Yet they know it not, and never once does it enter into their hearts. They go on at ease and are merry as if all were well, little thinking what is just before them in the judgment and pouring out of the wrath of God. What they consider just will be judged by Him.[22]

We need a word like this, both for ourselves as the church and for a world that is utterly persuaded of its own rectitude, but in truth is utterly indifferent to the holiness of God. The church has not confronted sinners with their sin precisely because it is permissive with itself. How, then, can it bring up the issue of their salvation?

Sinners awake! See what you are doing, where you are going. Consider what the end will be. Can your hands be strong or your heart endure, guilty rebel, when God Almighty shall come forth to deal with you according to your crimes? Now is the day of grace. God is ready to be reconciled. A door of mercy is opened by the blood of the Son of God. Pardon and peace are proclaimed to a rebellious and guilty world. Repent and be converted, that your sins may be blotted out.

If in all your hardness and impenitent heart you will venture to go on, treasuring up wrath against the day of wrath, you will know, to your everlasting sorrow that it is a fearful and horrible thing to sin against God. Against Thee, and

---

[22] *The Heinousness of Sin*

Thee only, have I sinned.[23]

In the cross of Christ, we see the wrath of God visited upon the Son of God. Imagine if the Son had not suffered it, so that the wrath of God fell upon the guilty. Mankind would be devastated both for time and eternity. Jesus received the cumulative wrath of mankind's sin in a six-hour travail of body and soul that was mercifully ended when He gave up His spirit. Why did God require His wrath to be expressed upon His Son? Can God be God, who is righteous and just, and not deal with the issue of sin? Surely He must demonstrate His horror and indignation toward the very thing that dishonors Him as God? If God were to diminish the issue of sin, or look the other way, mankind would be devoid of any consciousness of God as holy and righteous. Yet man can refuse the admonishment of God—for a time. When this happens, man's society becomes like Sodom and Gomorrah, wherein sin is celebrated and endorsed. And that society will have its end in much the same way that Sodom and Gomorrah ended—quickly, drastically, and disastrously.

The Father can rightfully ask any man, "What have you done with My Son? How have you understood His death?" Sin is a *willful* rejection of God, and nowhere is it more noticeable than the willful dismissal of the crucified Christ. If something this profound happens in history, and we dismiss it from our consideration, we are guilty of being unwilling to acknowledge God's statement about Himself. As hideous as the thought is, the Jewish people are especially without excuse. For the most part, they have looked upon Jesus as a misfit, a political reformer who jostled the Roman authorities, someone who was presumptuous about His credentials,

---

[23] Ibid.

and therefore suffered the unfortunate consequence.

God's provision for sinful mankind is that the agonizing, suffering death of His Son necessarily confronts us. Though He died for the sins of all mankind, we, individually, are not absolved from being the willful instruments in that death. Even though it was the best of Jewish religious piety and the best of Roman law that joined together to execute God, we are all implicated in that event. If that is what man is at his best, what then is he at his worst? It is what he is at his "best" that reveals the truth of his condition, especially when his condition makes him capable of murdering God. Man's "best" becomes his worst because it veils his inherent destitution.

The whole world lies in the power of Satan, the father of lies. The greatest lie he has perpetrated about the human condition is that there *is* such a thing as a man who is good, that we are not all that bad, and the "wrong" things we do cannot really be called sin. Satan deceives us about the truth of our own condition *as God sees it*. To reveal our condition, God first instituted redemptive sacrifices in which the blood of animals was spilled. The shedding of animal's blood, as mediated through priests, was to impress upon Israel the exceeding sinfulness of sin, requiring expiation through the shedding of blood: "Without shedding of blood there is no forgiveness."[24] Israel was made conscious of sin when they experienced the continual sacrifices, the rivers of blood, and finally the High Priest going into the holy of holies once a year for the atonement of the nation. Israel was steeped in this consciousness. God was preparing them for the Paschal Lamb who was going to take away the sins of the world, once and for

---

[24] Hebrews 9:22b. See Leviticus 17:11

all.

Even while mankind benefits from the atoning sacrifice of the Son, the *primary* purpose of the cross was for the Father's sake. Jesus died for mankind but, in a much more striking way, He died for God. The Father's honor was at stake. His name and character were being debased. Mankind, created in God's image, was continually slighting Him. How was God going to show His righteous, justified wrath against sin? The evil of sin required a demonstration as great as the terrible execution of His own Son; and the Son was willing to bear suffering unto death for His Father's sake. He died for God: for the name of God, the honor of God, the holiness of God. If God were to dismiss sin as something requiring a less serious judgment as that which fell upon His Son, then that raises questions about God: His integrity, the truth of His own character, and how He views sin and righteousness. God cannot allow sin to escape His judgment. It is a slight against Him. That is why His judgments are always acts of righteousness.

The fact that men have derived a salvation because of the shedding of God's blood is incidental to the greater purpose for that sacrifice. God is satisfied with the offering which He Himself provided. The smoking altar where an Israelite offered his lamb or his bullock not only testified that God could remit a person's sin, but declared also that God was holy. The whole issue of sacrifice from when it was first instituted, and finally in its ultimate expression, was not only to declare sin *as sin* and that man is guilty, but to declare that God is holy. Sacrifice is something that pertains to God's justice, to His sense of righteousness. God's holiness demands an answer to sin, or else God could be construed as being dismissive of sin.

Jesus taught the disciples to pray, "Our Father who is in heaven, hallowed be Your name."[25] Not only did He teach His disciples this prayer, He lived and died so that His Father's name would be hallowed. In entering the waters of the Jordan River, a picture of going down into death, Jesus was prefiguring His own crucifixion. His coming up out of the water was a foreshadowing of His resurrection. At that point, the voice of the Father rang out from heaven, "This is My beloved Son, in whom I am well-pleased."[26] In other words, "This is the Son who does not live for Himself; He is living for My name, for My honor. He hallows Me. His conduct, His sacrifice, His willing submission to death is in complete deference to Me, out of His love for Me as His Father."

To "hallow" is to honor as holy. But how many of us court the applause of men rather than the honor of the Father? What a different church we would be if we had God's name and honor as our first regard. Do our present actions glorify and exalt His name? Or do they, on the contrary, rob God's holiness from those who look upon our life and conduct? If we lived with the honor of God as the predominant motive of our lives, how much different would our life and witness be? And if Moses and David could fail in this, of what are *we* capable? How ought we to be conducting ourselves? We should always be conscious of the fact that these great men staggered and failed even though they knew that they were called to hallow God. It ought to encourage us toward a new seriousness, a new reverence for the holiness of God.

> What a fathomless depth of meaning He gave to the first petition in the Lord's Prayer, "Hallowed be thy name"! How God hates sin!...His honor

---

[25] Matthew 6:9b
[26] Matthew 3:17b

demanded the blood of the cross; how much more when He forgives it [sin]…In all time, past, present, or future, only those men are saved by the cross who believe; but equally in all time the cross honors God whether men believe it or not.[27]

To hallow the name of the Father cost Jesus His life. Can we hallow God, His honor and His reputation by our conduct and speech without paying for it through opposition, misunderstanding, or persecution? In a world at enmity with God, there will be a consequence for living to hallow God, for taking God seriously, for making Him our first priority over any other consideration. Living in ways that seek to step around or avoid this opposition, misunderstanding, or persecution is in effect to circumvent the cross.

---

[27] *The Epistle to the Romans* by James Stiffler, p. 65. Moody Press, 1960

CHAPTER 2

The Cross and the Holiness of God

God says that the priests shall teach the people the difference between the holy and the profane,[28] not only by proclamation, but by example. To profane is to turn what is holy into the commonplace. The sacred has got to be preserved and kept distinct from all that is common and unholy. This is the priestly function. If the priests do not know the difference, or are not careful to maintain the difference, how then shall the people know? Holiness is the essential attribute of God. There is no holiness apart from God. Any measure of holiness that we have is only the reflection of what has been wrought in us from His nature. No one else has it. If it were not for God, holiness would be absent from life and reality.

If we do not understand holiness, what does that say about our naiveté and optimism regarding the sinful nature of man? We can begin to see how hideous sin is by what was required and demonstrated in the magnitude of suffering by both the Father and the Son. Do we have an inward registration of the enormity of *that* fact? And is every aspect of our life and being

---

[28] See Ezekiel 44:23

affected by such?

As a willing "sin-bearer", Jesus suffered the judgment of God on sin. God's judgments are not arbitrary; they are in exact proportion to our sins. If the crucifixion of Jesus was the statement of God's wrath, what was the magnitude of the sin that Jesus willingly bore? He bore the physical devastation; He also bore the moral, psychological, emotional, and spiritual devastation. The forsakenness of the Father was more painful than what was visited upon His body. Being forsaken by the Father, with whom He had enjoyed eternal fellowship, was infinitely more painful than what was visited upon His body. He had to bear that because He became sin: "He made Him who knew no sin to be [become] sin on our behalf, so that we [who are sinful] might become the righteousness of God in Him."[29] God's righteous requirements must be met and satisfied, even if only He Himself can fulfill them. Righteousness requires a death for sin. Who could be a sin-bearer but one that is not corrupted and polluted by sin?

How many of us *prefer* to overlook our own sin? Our subjective assessment of ourselves is itself sin, and keeps us from any hope of knowing the exceeding sinfulness of sin. Yet, God does not let us subjectively determine either our own condition or the penalty for it. The cross was chosen by God for the display of His own holy character. To rightly look upon the crucified Christ is to see God's holiness, and will save us from any self-justifying lightness about our own unholy condition. If we do not have a right understanding of holiness as it is revealed in the character of God by the willing sacrifice of His own Son, and His own Son's willingness to bear that sacrifice, it will show itself in our own character and

---

[29] 2 Corinthians 5:21. Parentheses mine

in how we conduct ourselves throughout our life.

In observing the suffering of Jesus unto death, the Roman centurion concluded, "Truly this was the Son of God!"[30] Why were others who observed the same event unable to come to the same conclusion? It is recorded that many of the Jews responded with mocks and taunts: "He saved others; He cannot save Himself. He is the King of Israel; let Him now come down from the cross, and we will believe in Him."[31] They saw the same event as the centurion, but they responded in a totally different way. It was their sin that blocked out God's statement about Himself—in the same way our sin blocks out God's statement about Himself to us—and all the more condemning for them because they should have been the first to make that recognition, steeped as they were in the Law and the Prophets, both of which testified of Jesus. The Law and the Prophets as well testify that man's condition is helpless and hopeless apart from God. If we fail to see or acknowledge this truth, we affirm something about man that God denies. Those who agree with God that there is no hope for man in himself will see the heavens open. As we see Him *as He is*, we are changed and transformed from glory to glory.[32] We cannot see God and not be changed. Those who are not changed in the character of their lives are living statements testifying that they have not seen.

The Roman centurion would not likely have had much interest in the scriptural testimony about the human condition, yet God revealed something of Himself to this man that was not perceived by others who witnessed the same event. Though the centurion had seen numbers of men squirming, groaning, and

---

[30] Matthew 27:54
[31] Matthew 27:42
[32] See 2 Corinthians 3:18

cursing while being crucified, there was something about the manner of Jesus' dying that drew him to recognize His true identity. Though Jesus had performed many miracles, it was this decisive testimony of Himself—that is, the very manner of his dying—that brought what may well have constituted salvation for a man who otherwise would have eternally perished as a sinner.

The thief on a cross beside Jesus is another classic example of this paradox. He had likely joined the crowd of those who had been mocking Jesus, but then, reconsidering, he remonstrates with the other thief, recognizing that they deserve their punishment, and in so doing acknowledges that Jesus did not. He then says, "Jesus, remember me when You come in Your kingdom!"[33] What moved the thief to consider this writhing figure of humanity as the King of Glory, who had a kingdom that this dying man could actually enter into? In observing how Jesus departed this life, the thief received a revelation of a kingdom that was outside any Jewish category. There was something in Jesus' suffering unto death that was uniquely different from others he had seen die by crucifixion. Jesus forgave His executioners, and chose not to lay that sin to their charge. Jesus had a composure, a magnanimity and a grace in the manner in which He died. His legs did not have to be broken to shorten His agonizing lifespan. There was something exhibited of the majesty of the victim, not just because of His suffering, but *through* His suffering, that all the more illustrates who He is: the King of an eternal kingdom.

What keeps so many from this revelatory recognition? Would we be any more moved if we had

---

[33] Luke 23:42b

seen that fateful event in Jerusalem ourselves? What is there in us that blocks this breakthrough that God desires for all? There was sufficient evidence in what the criminal saw to save him, for Jesus' response to him so indicated: "Today you shall be with Me in Paradise."[34] Whatever was available in seeing ultimate truth in the suffering Christ is surely available for us.

In the Garden of Eden, we find that we all share in a nature typified by willful rebellion and defiance against God. In the first sin of Adam and Eve, we find all the constituent elements of *every* sin. God made only one request of Adam and Eve: that they could eat the fruit of any tree in the garden except for one tree. They violated that simple requirement in an obstinate, willful act as if they had the liberty to disregard God's command. It was as if they said to each other, "Even if God had said it, so what? Did He really mean it?" Satan raises questions about the character of God, disparaging God and His motives. God had not told Adam and Eve *why* they could not eat from that tree; He had told them that they *should* not. Eve accepted Satan's blasphemous assault upon the integrity of God—that is, she first entertained Satan's argument as a thought, validated that thought in her own heart, and then permitted the validated thought to compel her action. Why was she so susceptible to Satan's lie and questions raised about God's truth and character? Why could God not be implicitly believed and trusted?

In Eve's willingness to interact with Satan, in her failure to show horror at his suggestions, we see the process that preceded the act of eating the forbidden fruit. Here we have sin's true character. Sin proceeds from the heart and mind. Adam and Eve were drawn

---

[34] Luke 23:43b

away by their own lust, and then enticed into sin. Eve acquiesced when she should more rightly have been horrified. Where was Adam when he was allowing his wife to carry on the conversation? In allowing himself to be silent, he condoned and made himself one with that transgression. That is why both Eve *and* Adam were judged.

Sin is a deadly part of our human, Adamic nature. How many times have we given counsel when God is not requiring it? How often have we tried to comfort someone when God wants them to feel the full brunt of their condition? We can interfere with the sanctifying work of God even by our meddling. How often have we played the role of God and displaced God, not out of sinister intention but out of "good" intention? But it is still opposed to God.

> While a person may certainly be conscious of immoral acts and false motives, the reality of man's sinful state can never be perceived merely by self-knowledge. The totality and inclusiveness of Adam's sin and the consequent depravity of all mankind is an issue that is only truly made known in the cross.[35]

The writer strikes at the heart of the matter. To miss the deepest meaning of the cross is to lose the prospect of rightly comprehending our sinful and depraved condition. In the cross, we see the ultimate revelation of God's righteousness. In other words, the cross reveals the holiness of God and the depravity of man as no other single act of God is calculated to reveal. To fall short of apprehending the meaning of the cross *compounds* our sin, because it locks us into a subjective place of self-esteem by which we can never see the truth

---

[35] Source unknown

of our condition, nor seek God's remedy for it.

The only life that God approves, regards, or accepts comes out of death. True repentance, proceeding from a true revelation of God, *is* that death. But the sin of our self-righteousness keeps us from realizing and appropriating this desperately important provision. Paul wrote, "For I know that nothing good dwells in me, that is, in my flesh."[36] He distinguishes "in my flesh", which presupposes that he was aware that something good did dwell in him. But what is that good thing? Paul also wrote that he labored more abundantly than anyone else. In other words, the God of righteousness is bringing forth the fruit of righteousness through Paul, but Paul adds this critical qualifier, "and it is no longer I who live, but Christ lives in me."[37] The only righteousness that God is willing to accept is the righteousness that issues out of the nature of the Son who is formed in us.

Paul also wrote, "The sting of death is sin, and the power of sin is the Law."[38] How can the strength and power of sin derive from something as good as the Law? It is obviously not the Law itself; it is our presumption that convinces us there is something in man that can satisfactorily fulfill the Law. Could there be in us a post-Christian self-righteousness that is still operative, and even more tenacious, pervasive and continuing than ever we imagined? Is not our dullness toward the subject of sin and self-righteousness the very evidence of its existence? Why was our self-righteousness not dealt with at our conversion? *How deep was our conversion?* Did we at that time come to a full understanding and adoption of total disgust with our natural man, and a willingness to forsake "unto death"

---

[36] Romans 7:18a
[37] Galatians 2:20b
[38] 1 Corinthians 15:56

any attempt at our own righteousness? Was our water baptism a death and burial of our natural man because we knew there is no good that can come from it, or was our baptism just a scriptural requirement to which we felt obliged to submit to? If the latter, our self-righteousness surely remains.

"The sacrifice of the wicked is an abomination."[39] This verse implies that someone who lightly regards his own sin also believes that performing some perfunctory religious requirement is acceptable before God. If the person had avoided sacrifice, knowing that his condition required repentance before he dared bring an offering before God, it would not have been abominable. To bring a sacrifice in whatever form—to pray, to attend church, to worship—as if God does not see the truth of our condition makes it abominable. Cain was offended that God had not accepted his sacrifice. He could not understand why his brother's sacrifice was preferred and his was ignored. He esteemed himself out of all proportion to his true condition, which he soon revealed by murdering his own brother out of his resentment.

There is safety in continually keeping our hearts with all diligence. Be watchful for the leaven of sin, because a little leavens the whole lump. Be watchful for those first steps into sin. Be in the fellowship of believers frequently, so others can bring to your attention an aspect of sin you would not otherwise see. If we will not receive correction, the sin will enlarge and finally have its full outworking and consequence. If we are resentful when admonished, we will find ourselves committing a more grievous offense against God. We need to know how frail and vulnerable we are, even the best of us, and need to open ourselves to the provision of

---

[39] Proverbs 21:27

God to identify the subtleties of sin.

In the Book of Proverbs, Solomon warns us about relationships with ungodly women and foreign wives, but he himself later keeps a whole harem of foreign women. He thus contradicted his own holy calling. Who, then, is safe? We dare not criticize a fallen minister as if we are morally superior. To be continually broken before God and before others ought to be our normative posture.

True fellowship occurs between people related in and by truth. They are able to discern almost immediately where there is some kind of moral erosion for which a word of correction might be needed. To speak the truth in love does not mean speaking abstract biblical truths. It means speaking the truth to a brother or sister without exalting oneself, bringing correction in brokenness to the one who cannot see the blind spot. This aspect of true fellowship is not only for the sheep, but also for the shepherds. The notorious failings of shepherds in our generation are a statement that they themselves have not submitted to, or been accessible for correction that ought to have come to them from their own sheep. True fellowship is as much God's provision for the shepherd as for the sheep. The sinful downfall of an elder is an indictment against the fellowship for its failure to identify the first signs of sin and to bring correction. Either that or they were totally oblivious to it in their human admiration for the man; and therefore they were unwilling to address him in his own defect.

True fellowship brings a measure of obligation from each one of us. Our ability to discern is relative to the truth of our own conduct—that is, the degree to which our own life conforms to Truth. If we are dulled through our own indulgences, our moral lapses, how then shall we discern the condition and need of another?

And if we do not have the courage to speak to a brother in love, it shows we are deferring to man rather than hallowing the name of the Lord. This is *not* an invitation to "roast" everyone in the fellowship. The church is called to speak the truth in love so that we might come to the place of maturity in all aspects. We are called to active involvement in each other's lives, requiring humility, love, truth, and a sense of holiness.

Is there a day in which we are not transgressing by some initiative of our own? Each day has its own complexities in which there is always opportunity, in one way or another, to express something opposed to God. The vilest form of sin is when we oppose God *in the name of God*; when we are trafficking in God, enlisting God's name to sanctify and validate something that has come out of our own flesh: "God said that I am to...God told me that..." It is a despicable form of transgression to sanctify our carnality and self-will by invoking God's name. The flesh is always at enmity with God, always wanting to express its carnal thoughts.

We should be praying every morning, "Lord, forgive me my transgressions even though I am not conscious of any. Iniquity is ever ready to rise up within me. It might be something inadvertent, and though I may not be conscious of it, or can identify it, Lord, I am asking Your forgiveness for it. Keep my transgressions ever before me; never let me forget how they offend You."

CHAPTER 3

The Crucifixion of Jesus

Victims of crucifixion proliferated the highways in the days of the Roman Empire. It was the primary form of execution for rebellious slaves, a deterrent to keep other slaves subservient. It was the most degrading form of execution. The victim died a horribly painful death, lingering on at times for three or more days. Crucifixion combined the death penalty with excruciating torture and total humiliation. Being nailed, naked, to a wooden post conferred the greatest possible indignity, with the victim writhing in agony and shame right to the end. The flogging that preceded the crucifixion sapped the victim's strength, thereby shortening the time of torturous death. The executioners would finally break the legs of the victims so they would stop pushing themselves up to get their breath; then they would asphyxiate as the body fluids in their lungs drowned them. Crucifixion was an utterly gruesome business, cruel and sadistic. It is hardly surprising that the Jewish historian, Josephus, described it as the most wretched of deaths.

In Colmar, France, there is a remarkable painting entitled "The Isenheim Altar" by the 16th century artist,

Matthias Grünewald. There are many depictions of Jesus, but none as shocking as this. The artist paints the crucifixion in all of its ugliness, brutality, and shame. It shows a man in the final stages of death: devastated, battered, and bruised. His head hangs down upon His chest. His mouth is parted. His eyes are sunken deep in the skull. His lips are white and encrusted with saliva around the edges. His face bears the imprint of the final paroxysm of suffering. His body, flecked with coagulated blood, has a greenish, gangrenous hue from the flagellations He received. Splinters protrude from His flesh. His fingers and feet are stretched out and misshapen. One can hardly imagine anything more deathly looking. Rightly did Isaiah prophesy that He would be "marred more than any man."[40]

The artist depicted Jesus with a loincloth, but there is no historical evidence to support that claim. Artists have no inhibition with displaying the blood caused by the crown of thorns and the flogging, but they have shrunk from portraying the nakedness of Christ. The artistic addition of a modest loincloth conceals the shame that was an integral part of crucifixion: namely, the nakedness of the victim, stripped of his clothing, with arms nailed to the cross, and therefore unable to cover himself. Why would God send His Son to suffer the most barbaric form of punishment men could devise?

The victims of the cross were flogged mercilessly in preparation for the actual crucifixion. They would then have to carry the wooden beam on backs that had been slashed to the bone. It would have been excruciatingly painful. One could almost say that the physical death was a relief from the pain they had already undergone.

---

[40] Isaiah 52:14

They would be subjected to verbal abuse, taunts, and mocking from those who would watch the execution. We need to be jabbed in our deeps lest we trivialize Jesus' suffering and sentimentalize it, which is just as effective in negating its importance as to disregard it.

Jesus bore this unspeakable humiliation, the public display of His private parts, so that we, because of that, may not be compromised in that area. He was wounded in the head for our thought life, so that we would not let our thoughts roam about at our own will and desire. His hands were pierced for our evil practices, for which reason many of us cannot yet lay holy hands upon others and send them forth into the purposes of God. He was wounded in the feet, because we have carried our bodies to places where they ought not to have been. These are symbolic humiliations and penetrations upon His body occasioned by the way we—each one of us—have thought, spoken, acted, and lived.

How many of us have realized that what Jesus demonstrated on the cross is at the heart of the gospel? Paul could say that he was not ashamed of the gospel of Jesus Christ. He knew experientially that there was a power inherent in the gospel to save anyone willing to bring themselves into a believing identification with the shame of the cross. Paul knew the magnitude of sin in which every human soul abides. He knew that the wages of sin is death—an eternal separation from God, an eternal anguish of soul that would be without remedy. Therefore, Paul was not ashamed of the very thing that would save mankind from that irremediable torment. On the other hand, if we do not understand the magnitude of sin and the wrath of God upon sin, then we *will* be ashamed and offended by the gospel. The suffering of Christ can only do its redemptive work when we see it in the context of what is required to expiate and expunge sin from our earthly bodies.

Jesus willingly submitted to this form of suffering unto death in order that we would not hide and cover ourselves, that we would be as willing, in some measure, to be openly and publicly exposed in the things that are humiliating. If we refuse, if we shrink away, we will not receive the benefit of God's grace and redemptive work that waits upon the acknowledgment of the truth of our condition. If we, in our pride, cover and conceal because we do not want to be exposed, we forfeit that grace. God wants to meet us in the naked truth of our condition as He sees it.

What is it about human nature that wants to remove the sting of the cross? Why do we prefer to make of it a theology, or devise and live by our own humanly formulated "principles" of the faith? We can speak profusely about atonement and even sing, "He was wounded for our transgressions", but the conduct of our lives continues to betray the fact that we have not been transformed by this radical statement made by God about Himself. If we ever needed light from heaven, it is here. Nothing else will give us a horror for sin. Nothing else will keep us from crucifying the Son of God afresh than to really understand what God suffered in humiliation and unspeakable degradation at the hands of men.

Suffering reveals truth as nothing else can. Suffering gets right to the heart of the issue, lays it bare, and reveals things as they really are. God suffered unspeakable shame in order that we should be shameless before Him. He came nakedly into the world and He died nakedly. This was God who came down to earth, imprisoned in the humiliating form of a man, who was born into the world as a helpless, dependent infant. He laid aside His glory, lived a life of obscurity, suffered the rejection of His people, and His life ended in an unspeakable torture, about which the scriptures simply say: "And they crucified Him."[41] Even God does not attempt to describe the awful suffering of that death.

> But He was pierced through for our transgressions, He was crushed for our iniquities; the chastening for our well-being fell upon Him, and by His scourging we are healed. All of us like sheep have gone astray, each of us has turned to his own way; but the LORD has caused the iniquity of us all to fall on Him.[42]

If we want to know how horrendous sin is in God's sight, then see and ponder the Son of God nakedly hanging in excruciating suffering. Has the horror of sin struck us to the point where we shudder at the thought of sin? We are living in an age that abounds with iniquity, with lust, powerful seductions and subtle sensualities. Only those who have laid the cross to their self-life will be safe. They have recognized the evil propensities of their flesh. They know that self-conscious discipleship is not the answer, that human determination is not the answer. They know that a true, continuous, ever-present understanding, appreciation, and application of the cross of Christ, the place of suffering and shame, are the only answer.

Jesus says to His followers, "Take up your cross and follow Me." Of what then shall we be too proud if God Himself suffered this? He suffered it to reveal the depth of our pride in order that we would not have any ground to stand upon by which we keep ourselves from a necessary humbling. If God will suffer that humiliation and public exposure, should we not also be

---

[41] Mark 15:24
[42] Isaiah 53:5-6

willing to follow Him in that same humiliation? If we keep ourselves guarded and protect ourselves from any loss of our own dignity, we cannot rightly be called His disciples. How disrespectful toward God when we retain our pride! God will be diminished in the eyes of others; His reputation—*His name*—will suffer loss. Authentic Christian lives are established in suffering and humiliation rather than out of some flamboyant ability of our own.

Is there anything more distasteful than false humility? We can only have true humility to the measure we are in union with God, who Himself is humble by nature, and have joined Him in the fellowship of His humiliating sufferings. We are the continuation, so to speak, of what He began in His own suffering and death. In the school of humiliation, in the dealings of God, in being found out, we are not to hide, conceal, or depict ourselves as something other than flesh and blood men and women.

We take up our cross knowing that we are going to a place of ultimate suffering and humiliation unto death. The cross is the only instrument upon which our natural man, our self-life is put to death. It is only on this true and ultimate ground that the sanctifying work of God can take place. Jesus makes it very clear that to follow Him, to be counted as one of his disciples is the willingness to be exposed and open before God, which means being open and exposed before each other. In this kind of relationship, we can trust one another so that we might receive the prayer, the correction, and the encouragement available only in an environment of this kind.

If we are earnest in our daily walk, we will continually find ourselves in circumstances that call us to the cross. If we are not experiencing daily suffering because of our identification with Christ, it is because we are shrinking from the cross; we are protecting our dignity, our self-life. We see so little resurrection reality in the lives of God's people because we see so little "death" reality. There is a daily dying and a daily rising only if we are walking in earnestness with the Lord. The cross puts to death both the worst aspects of our nature and our best, because even our best can never be good enough in God's sight. It is still all too human, shot through with sin and ego, vanity and pride. It can never serve God in a priestly way. There will always be a self-serving aspect so long as any root of the natural man remains. A frequent meditation of the cross would be a wonderful antidote for our sham and falsity.

When I survey the wondrous cross
On which the Prince of glory died,
My richest gain I count but loss,
And pour contempt on all my pride.

Forbid it, Lord, that I should boast,
Save in the death of Christ, my God.
All the vain things that charm me most,
I sacrifice them to His blood.

See, from His head, His hands, His feet,
Sorrow and love flow mingled down.
Did e'er such love and sorrow meet,
Or thorns compose so rich a crown?[43]

---

[43] Isaac Watts (1674-1748), English hymn writer.

If you walk round to the back of Grünewald's masterpiece, the artist has painted the resurrection of Jesus. It shows Jesus coming out of the tomb as the glorified Christ with His arms outstretched. Brilliant beams of glory pour out of every place where He had been punctured and wounded. As ugly as the crucifixion was, it cannot compare with the glorious resurrection. This is God demonstrating Himself, both in humiliation and in exaltation. This is the Pattern Son, and He bids us to follow Him, to share in His sufferings, and then to enter with Him into glory.

CHAPTER 4

The Cross as Suffering

Though it seems to contradict what we may think God is, or desire God to be, a crucified God is at the heart of the Christian faith. Our every imagined notion of what *we* would think God ought to be needs itself to be crucified in the context of that greater crucifixion. But the terrible irony is that we can take this event and make of it a commonplace. We can form a doctrine about it and lose its reality for exactly that very reason.

If we suffer from a faulty image of God, we will have an equally faulty image of ourselves. More than we know, our view of God is the projection or expression of our view of ourselves. The two views are inexorably joined. In other words, we will never see ourselves as we truly are until we see God as He truly is. When we prefer a more honorable view of God than a crucified God, we are in fact, elevating what we think is honorable in man. Isaiah's cry, "Woe is me, for I am ruined,"[44] is altogether an appropriate response to seeing and receiving God *as He is* rather than what we suppose Him to be. Those who have no regard for a dehumanized, crucified Christ do so because He

---

[44] Isaiah 6:5

contradicts all their ideas of God and man.

If we think that we can grow in the faith by conceptualizing it, or formulating "correct principles" of the faith, we are, ourselves, alienated from true reality. God is not a concept. He cannot be formulated as an idea in our mind. Such attempts will inevitably result in making man and his mind superior to the God who is being formulated. God is beyond our human categories to conceptualize Him.

The cross demolishes all concepts of who we think God to be. Will we surrender to the truth of God in the form that He is pleased to give? If we choose to ignore or reject the statement that God gave of Himself, and view Him instead on the basis of our own concepts, the end of that is an elevation of man at the expense of God. Furthermore, we pay greatly for our unwillingness to see and to consider the truth of God in the crucifixion of Jesus. Faith comes from "hearing the word of Christ."[45] That is, hearing the word of the crucified Christ, the very foundation of the reality of God for the salvation of men.

The central theme by which those in the world live their lives is the avoidance of pain and the pursuit of pleasure. To remove oneself from that mode of life always results in a rupture. There is an enormous distance between heaven and earth, between God and man, between time and eternity, between the way of the world and the way of the cross. The only means by which the reality of the one will make way for the other must, of necessity, occasion a suffering. The cross is the statement of an intrinsic, necessary suffering; the fixed, unswerving principle of God found at the heart of all true reality. Unless the place of suffering has registered

---

[45] Romans 10:17b

deeply in our consciousness and we have been apprehended by it—that is, unless the reality and meaning of the cross in revealing the truth of God has arrested the progress of our natural self-life—we cannot rightly lay claim to being the people of God. The Lord knows those who are His; and that knowing is conditioned by our appropriation of, and adherence to, the purpose of the crucifixion of Jesus.

The most intense forms of pain and suffering will invariably come to us from the very people who are our nearest and dearest. If it came from unregenerate people, we could more easily bear it. When it comes from our own household, our loved ones, and those in our fellowship, we begin to taste something of suffering in its most intense forms. Perhaps any suffering less intense than this cannot bring the chastening depth of work that God is after. God knows what we need. Those people who are opposing us are actually serving His purposes in our formation as His sons and daughters. If we can understand the sanctifying work of God, then it saves us from seeing the brethren, or our spouses, as our "enemies." We will see them in a more redemptive way and have a more sympathetic view of a suffering that they must bear until the purposes of God are outworked. In the seemingly intractable, insoluble oppositions and differences, we have simply to bear with them. The Lord Himself, in His time, will bring the release when the work in us has been accomplished. In the meantime, we can expect to feel what seems like "hell's fury" directed against us. It is an anguish that needs to be borne.

A sculptor does not use a manicure set to reduce the crude, unshapely marble into a thing of beauty. The saw, the hammer, and the chisel are crude tools, but without them the rough stone must remain forever formless and unbeautiful. To do His supreme work of grace within you, He will take from within your heart everything you love most; everything you trust in will go from you. Piles of ashes will lie where your most trusted treasures used to be.[46]

Redemptive suffering is a form of death. Paul spoke of a daily dying, a death working in him that would work life in those whose lives he touched. Every true servant, having a jealousy for God's glory, will taste death on a daily basis. In the purposes of God, it may mean disappointment to those who thought that you were going to be the answer to their predicament. When Jesus heard that His friend Lazarus was sick, He did not rush to his bedside to preserve that natural physical life. Instead, He remained longer where He was, sufficient for that life to die.

So the sisters sent word to Him saying, "Lord, behold, he whom You love is sick." But when Jesus heard this, He said, "This sickness is not to end in death, but for the glory of God, so that the Son of God may be glorified by it."[47]

The Son of God's passion for the glory of God overshadowed the need to bring immediate comfort to His sick friend. There will always be a price to pay for those who share this priority. What anguish of soul are we willing to suffer for that glory? We should not minimize how much Lazarus himself suffered. He would have been writhing with fever, waiting for Jesus to come through the door and heal him; but it never happened. Lazarus would have likely died in terrible

---

[46] *That Incredible Christian: How Heaven's Children Live on Earth* by A.W. Tozer, page 122, compiled by Anita M. Bailey and published by Christian Publications, Camp Hill, PA. in 1964
[47] John 11:3-4

disappointment. His sisters, Martha and Mary, would also have been in anguish of soul, having to bear the painful disappointment of not seeing Jesus come to heal their brother. Jesus would have borne the disappointment of his friends without the freedom to explain His actions to them. To suffer misunderstanding is made all the more acute when it comes from those who are closest to you.

And beyond these disappointments, Jesus would have borne the inevitable reproaches of His disciples, their misunderstanding and critical looks. There was no attempt to explain His actions, only the cryptic, mysterious statement, "This sickness is not to end in death, but for the glory of God, so that the Son of God may be glorified by it." What could those words have meant to His disciples? Unless we are intensely jealous for the glory of God, we will not be able to stand reproach when it comes. We will find ourselves condescending to man, acting out of self-interest, doing the conventional and religious thing; and thereby saving ourselves.

When Jesus came to Bethany, He was reproved by *both* sisters: "Lord, if You had been here, my brother would not have died."[48] The crisis of their brother's death revealed that their concern for his life was a higher priority than their jealousy for the glory of God. Jesus answered them: "Did I not say to you that if you believe, you will see the glory of God?"[49]

To show true love may well mean withholding immediate relief from distress, even from those who are near and dear to us. In fact, what is the love of the Father toward us? Is it saving us from being hurt and

---

[48] Ibid., v.21b and v.32
[49] Ibid., v.40b

keeping us from trial and difficulty? Such was not the case between the Father and the Son. No, that would be a self-serving and sparing love, which we often see expressed by parents toward their children and even pastors toward their congregations. However, the Father chastises those whom He loves by allowing affliction rather than release from it, because there is something of a greater and redemptive kind at stake.

It is the prospect of suffering in whatever form, be it shame, or humiliation, or embarrassment that intimidates us. How many of our rationales and justifications, by which we keep ourselves from fellowship with God's people, really originate because we are afraid of the exposure? We are afraid to be found out, afraid to fail before the eyes of others, afraid to suffer humiliation. Is there anything more mortifying than to stand at the tomb of Lazarus and cry out in obedience, "Come forth!" without anything happening? Are we willing to experience *that*? The definition of an obedient son is one who does not prematurely act out of his own natural humanity and compassion. Such a one has no desire to alleviate suffering and allows death to have its full course so that there might be a resurrection from the dead that will glorify God.

Our capacity to bear the sufferings of Christ is the true index of our spirituality. Any form of Christianity that is painless, that seeks to avoid tension, that wants to assure us of comfort, that provides pleasant services and programs, may well be a statement of Christian apostasy. To shield ourselves from pain is to keep us from the very thing that would encourage reality: namely, the true knowledge of God Himself.

Suffering should not be looked upon as something grim, experienced only by those who are alienated from God. There is a redemptive purpose inherent in a suffering that is borne *for righteousness' sake*. We do not have to seek out suffering in a self-inflicting way. The sufferings of Christ were of a particular kind; a kind which came as the *consequence* of His obedience. Suffering will come to us in our lives in a redemptive way out of the logic of a life rightly lived in God. "Indeed, all who desire to live godly in Christ Jesus will be persecuted."[50] The fact that so many in the church shun and avoid suffering, failing to understand its centrality, is the very evidence that we do not have a "cross-consciousness." For us, the cross has become something other than God's intention: namely, a harmless thing, a safe thing, a timid thing, an adornment. It is the final logic—and will be the ultimate condemnation—of a church that has opted for the world's values rather than the way of God.

There is a conscious moment of reckoning when the cross is moved from abstract consideration to a point at which our lives are consecrated to its sanctifying work; when we have surrendered to the necessary truth of the inevitable suffering inherent in the faith. To make our peace with the cross is to surrender to this truth. Only then will we be released for the very things that promote our maturity and sonship.

Embracing the cross will mean daily humiliations. There will be painful recognitions and revelations about us that will need our attention. The suffering of humiliation was demonstrated by the Lord Himself at the cross. To miss *this* meaning of the cross is to miss it everywhere. It is to live a distorted and unrealistic spiritual life, being subject to deception and every kind of fad that circulates in Christian ministries. The cross is the place of sanity, reality, and truth—at the heart of

---

[50] 2 Timothy 3:12

58

which are pain and suffering; necessary preludes to ushering in the glory of God.

If the cross is not willingly embraced, salvation is reduced to a human formula rather than divine reality. We see this in the way that a man-deferring gospel characterizes much of modern-day evangelism. We all have heard the statement: "God has a plan for your life." This is an appeal to man's fulfillment and gratification rather than the true recognition of ourselves as God sees us. If people come to the faith by "accepting Jesus" in a decisional way, then falsity, distortion, and deception will be the result. In other words, when the *beginning* is not centered in the cross, the outworking is going to be self-centeredness and egotism, glossed over with spiritual terminology. It is a lesser "gospel", a religion of convenience, one that does not make any requirement of us. Ours becomes a pseudo-Christian culture having no more validity in the world than any other religion. We become as salt that has lost its savor.

Jesus was the Lamb crucified from the foundation of the world. There was something that had to be worked out in creation that could not be performed in any other way. The crucifixion of Jesus was not some lamentable happenstance, nor a solution to some "mistake" made by God. The holy self-sacrifice of God should not be turned into a piece of merchandise whereby melancholy souls receive gratification. This is a sickly form of sentimentalizing the cross that reinforces the self-life and makes the crucified Jesus an object of pity, which is in reality only an extension of our own self-pity.

Self-pity is one of the greatest curses of modern life. The world languishes in it. God's great antidote is the cross. The cross should make of us dead men, and we all know what happens when one sticks a dead man with a pin. Where is there room for self-pity when we contemplate the crucified God? The cross is the healthiest life-giving provision for sanity, right living, and relationship that we are offered in life. Seeing Christ and Him crucified takes us out of ourselves, our self-pity, our moaning and groaning about life's misfortunes. We have a wonderful provision in the woundedness of the Lord Himself to heal and deliver us from what otherwise would have robbed us of health and life. The cross, rightly perceived and rightly applied, is a wonderful emancipation from becoming unduly preoccupied with our own hurts. To contemplate and rightly see the wounds of Jesus is to dismiss any preoccupation with the wounds *we* may have suffered. If we have any intention in God, we should fully expect to experience rejection, opposition, persecution, pain, misery, suffering, and even physical death. The cross is God's provision to remove from us any cowardice. The Lord Himself has given us a standard, and the courage of His life, to fulfill the obedience to which He calls us. As *He* drank His cup, so too have we to drink our own.

Moltmann rightly noted that the more Christianity becomes the acceptable religion of prevailing society, the more the brutality of the cross becomes gilded with other, differing expectations and ideas of salvation. It is interesting that German society despised the brutality of the cross because it showed Christ "dehumanized." They did not see that the cross was God's provision to save them from the brutality of their own nature by His suffering brutality at the hands of mankind. Those who were most offended came from the German middle-class, bourgeois, liberal, rationalist civilization of the 18th and 19th centuries. This was where so much of reformed Judaism was birthed. Germany then brutalized and inflicted upon the Jewish people, and others, the most dehumanizing of all sufferings and deaths: namely, the Nazi Holocaust. They dehumanized their victims with brutality and degradation by giving them a number rather than a name, by stripping them of anything that had to do with human decency. In the end, they became the very thing they rejected. If we are going to be saved from the brutality of our own human nature, we need to receive what was brutally inflicted upon Jesus. The degree to which we take offense at this fact is the measure of our sin and self-elevation; we are too proud to recognize what our condition is before God, and what it required of Him in His suffering and death to expiate sin.

Moltmann reminds us that Jesus incited His enemies against Himself by His message and the life that He lived. He suffered for righteousness' sake. We might just as well be speaking about the apostle Paul. Obedience to the heavenly vision brought him into prisons, into shipwrecks, into beatings, into rejection. The scandal of western Christianity has been the absence of this suffering. Something is not taking place; we are not living in that same obedience, and, therefore, we have been shielded from its resulting suffering. Our willingness to follow the Lord and take up our cross daily will have consequences for us in this life. The cross is never a once-and-for-all event; it is something we face daily. Every moment of the day, an issue of the cross will always be before us. We will always have the choice of sparing ourselves the suffering of shame and humiliation or to submit to it in humble obedience.

A Christian life that is not cross-centered is not a Christian life. There is a fundamental reckoning that each of us needs to face, where we throw in the towel and say, "Yes, Lord, I recognize now as I have never before understood it. The cross is not some sideline. It is the heart of the matter, and I don't know that I have ever really made my peace with it, or if I have ever really surrendered to the truth that suffering is inexorable, that it is intrinsic to the Christian life. And as I survey myself, I know that I find ways to dodge and avoid the humiliation of the cross. Right now, I'm going to give up that dodging and avoidance and live a life that is surrendered to the cross, to the truth of it. And let whatever is ordained by You to come to me in Your unique formation of my life."

The sacrament of water baptism is valid only when undertaken with this measure of surrender. How many would choose to be baptized with this kind of understanding? To make one's peace with the cross, in *that* understanding, is in effect to have come to the cross. It is one thing to discuss the cross, and even examine it, but *have we come to it*? And when we do, we will receive its efficacy and benefit beyond the issue of atonement for sin. The cross is the place of deliverance, the place of true reality. The cross has an inherent power to free us when we have come to it in truth; when we understand what it represents and surrender to that truth. Taking up of our daily cross will follow. A foundational decision needs to be made, or we never will come into that place of true reality.

CHAPTER 5

The Cross – God Revealed

The cross is ruthless and absolute. It is a straight, unswerving standard to which everything in our lives should conform, against which everything must be measured. If the work of the cross is absent or has been neglected in our lives, and some other substitute has been put in its place that is not the cross of the crucified Christ, then *everything* that constitutes the truth and reality of God is going to be distorted. And if we are too glib in expressing knowledge of the cross, or we seem to have neatly nailed it down and can quote statements about it, then in all probability we have missed its deepest meaning.

When our voices are filled with the praises of God, and our emotions are aroused by the mention of the name of Jesus, to what degree are we celebrating the crucified and risen Christ? To what degree are we, instead, singing our songs to a blurred image of our own making that serves our own self-interest and well-being? Instead of God forming us into His image, many of us are guilty of forming God into *our* image, which in turn produces a vacuous Christianity void of truth or power. A projection takes place in our minds when we hear the name of Jesus mentioned. Every one of us has a variation on who we think Jesus is. If the picture of Jesus formed in our mind is any other than He who was crucified and rose again, then it is a "Jesus" who likely serves our own needs and ends rather than the sacrificial Lamb of God. To see Jesus as a deity who serves our purposes completely contradicts the Christ who suffered and died. If God is to correct our image of Himself, which means also correcting the image we have of ourselves, then the only place where it can be done is at the cross. We need to know God *exactly* as He is. That knowledge is nowhere presented more accurately than in His suffering unto death. The cross, therefore, is the very place where the profoundest capacity to reveal the truth of God can be found.

In the final analysis, everything that leads to the fragmentation of human society stems from the failure to radically apprehend God as He in fact is and as He desires to be known. If we, like Paul, were to determine to know nothing but a crucified Christ as the foundation of our faith and walk, we would not give our minds to the kinds of subjectivities and self-imaginings—especially about God—to which we are prone.

> Now from the sixth hour darkness fell upon all the land until the ninth hour. About the ninth hour Jesus cried out with a loud voice, saying, "ELI, ELI, LAMA SABACHTHANI?" that is, "MY GOD, MY GOD, WHY HAVE YOU FORSAKEN ME?"[51]
>
> And Jesus cried out again with a loud voice, and yielded up His spirit. And behold, the veil of the

---

[51] Matthew 27:45-46

> temple was torn in two from top to bottom; and
> the earth shook and the rocks were split.[52]

When Jesus was impaled upon the cross, a great darkness came over the earth. This "darkness" must come upon us also; a negation of *all* things, even those things which we think we have understood about the cross. How many of us would be willing for that kind of darkness and utter destitution of soul to come upon us, even to the point where the doctrines of which we are so assured should all be brought to nothing? Though the things we speak of might be true, for many of us, they have not been *made* true in our lives. They cannot be made true until we allow this darkness to come over us. God is waiting for us to divest ourselves of mere biblical phrases and be willing to suffer a "dark night" of the soul in order for us to come into a true knowledge of Himself.

In the daytime of our comfortable religious understanding, all must go dark for us and become as night. We have become too casual about the cross, and have made of it only a theory, a formula for salvation. We have come to altar calls, responding to invitations to "lay down our lives before Christ" or "accept Jesus into our hearts" again and again; yet our self-life is still very much alive. The veil of selfishness, self-interest, vanity and pride is still not rent. Our rocky hearts are still not split. Why has the revelatory event of the cross of Christ, the true revealing of God, not taken place in our lives?

> But we do see Him...namely, Jesus, because of the suffering of death crowned with glory and honor.[53]

---

[52] Ibid., vv.50-52
[53] See Hebrews 2:9

To see Him as He is means also to see ourselves as we are. To have a distorted notion of Him is to exist with an equally distorted and self-exalting notion of ourselves. To see Jesus in His suffering is to see the most accurate depiction of God as He truly is. To see Jesus in that condition is to see the glory of God. Are we willing to abandon everything in order to see Him as He is? When we see Him as He in fact is, there is nothing left to do but to repent from our self-centered existence and from lives that bear little correspondence with His sacrificial one. Only then can true faith emerge. How many of us are valiantly seeking to avoid coming into the true knowledge of God, willing to experience seeming "abandonment," where all that we cherished has perished, where we are bereft even of what we thought we understood the faith to be? How many of us have misunderstood the circumstances that God brings into our lives to press us toward the true knowledge of Him?

Nothing less than the cross can separate us from a world that is powerfully seductive and at enmity with God. Do our hearts wince when we touch any aspect of the spirit and wisdom of this world? Is its wisdom as abominable to us as it is to God, not only in its ugliest vices, but also in those things applauded as virtuous and good but which are equally of the world? "That which is highly esteemed among men is detestable in the sight of God."[54] Do we treat the world as if it is under the judgment of God? Do we see *all* of its aspects, including its culture and the things that are imposing, elegant and honorific, as also having their origin in hell, being ruled over by the prince of darkness? Is our distaste for the world such that we cannot wait to get out of it? Do we see ourselves as pilgrims and strangers

---

[54] Luke 16:15b

looking for a city not made with hands? Could our inordinate fascination for the world and its ways testify to the fact that we have tragically avoided the cross? Paul could say that he boasted only in the cross of Christ, through which the world had been crucified to him, and he to the world.[55] That the world can so easily tolerate us without reproach and persecution is itself a shameful testimony that we are so like the world that we cannot be distinguished from it. Despite the things that we verbally profess, our lives are lived as if God did not exist. We ought rather to be citizens of another kingdom, citizens of heaven. There is no way to attain to such citizenship without the work of the cross of Christ.

At a time when the church should be preparing herself to be a visible place of refuge in a coming age of conflict and calamity, an island of sanity and reality in a sin-soaked world, she herself seems to be largely occupied with the spirit of this world. She is producing a new breed of super executives, slick promoters, and multi-million dollar facilities that often elicit the admiration of the world...but have no message for it. Weary millions tramp about in a no man's land of religious frustration and defeat, professing doctrines that are more cerebral and credal than real, while legalism abounds in the very name of grace.

In the unreality that pervades many of our church services, we are unconsciously yielding more and more to worldly methods of conduct. What can a pastor do with a carnal congregation that brings into the meetings its dead weight? If he wants to have a "successful" service, he will find himself yielding more and more to a spirit of manipulation in order to produce some

---

[55] See Galatians 6:14

semblance of spiritual life. Manipulation is the antithesis of faith. It is a scandal and a shame that many of our services (particularly in the Charismatic and Pentecostal realm) resemble high school football rallies. In pumping up flesh, they are thinking it is the deepest spirituality. How many of us are willing to consider that this may well be an avoidance of the cross? Or are we quite comfortable with that environment?

If we waited on God in silence, it would reveal the truth of our spiritual bankruptcy. Whether we are conscious of it or not, we show a marked tendency to want to drown out our superficiality with our noise, our amplifiers, and our ceaseless activity. There is often an unspoken agreement between ministers and congregations by which the "show goes on" for the preservation of a safe *status quo*, even while carnality and sin abound, unchecked and unaddressed, in the lives of both the congregants and the ministers. In the name of defending the faith, fearful and cowardly shepherds find themselves ironically opposing or denigrating it in their ignorance. The spontaneity of the leading of the Holy Spirit hardens into a fixed liturgy of choruses, followed by dramatic pauses, and, depending upon where you are, pontifical prophecies that are of a most general kind, words one would hardly expect God to speak. They are accepted for the nothing things that they are, and we go right on with "business as usual" without being in any way affected. Such "services" have become mere performance and entertainment, and our lack of concern is the proof of what our real attitude is. In the avoidance of the cross of Christ, our contemporary church life is really not much more than a Christian culture, a vacuous praise club, attributing gain as godliness; a comfortable religiosity that leaves our real interests unchallenged and undisturbed.

The denial of self in any form is a painful suffering. Many of us are unable and unwilling to face the issue of its pain. If anyone were to walk into our church services, our heads automatically turn to look; we *must* be seeing; we *must* be hearing something; silence cannot be tolerated; our minds *must* be engaged; our fingers *must* be occupied. Paul wrote, "For I determined to know nothing among you except Jesus Christ, and Him crucified."[56] It is amazing how our intellect likes to *know* many things just for the sake of knowing. To deny our mind the pleasure of contemplating what it chooses is an exercise in suffering. Any act of self-denial is an exercise in suffering. We need to encourage one another to welcome the inherent centrality of suffering as being part and parcel of normative Christian living. Jesus' character, life and message made inevitable His own death at the hands of unregenerate mankind. What then shall be brought upon us if we desire to be formed into His character, move in His life, and proclaim His message?

Jesus said, "If anyone wishes to come after Me, he must deny himself, and take up his cross and follow Me."[57] For those who hear that call, the cross is the power of God as expressed in resurrection life. Having already come once, we invite upon ourselves the daily dying, the daily reiteration of this mystery in ways that are uniquely appropriate to our lives, our call and our walk. If the cross is not operative daily, if we are not willing to suffer its deaths, then we make ourselves also, to that degree, candidates for sin and deception.

Being saved from deception is the issue of the cross. Are we willing to be ruthless with regard to ourselves, bearing the humiliation of a defect in ourselves when

---

[56] 1 Corinthians 2:2
[57] Matthew 16:24b

God makes it clear to us? If we run from confrontation, if we rationalize and justify our conduct, finding a way to explain it that satisfies us and saves us from the acknowledgement of sin as sin, then we are avoiding the cross and God's redemptive answer for us. We need to be lovers of truth. The most acute expression of truth is Christ and Him crucified. The individual who moves away from the cross, who is not willing for the suffering of the cross, not willing to live the cruciform life, is not a lover of truth. And in the days to come, such avoidance may occasion eternal death, for as Paul says in 2 Thessalonians 2: 8-10:

> Then that lawless one will be revealed whom the Lord will slay with the breath of His mouth and bring to an end by the appearance of His coming; that is, the one whose coming is in accord with the activity of Satan, with all power and signs and false wonders, and with all deception of wickedness for those who perish because they did not receive the love of the truth so as to be saved. For this reason God will send upon them a deluding influence so that they will believe what is false, in order that they all may be judged who did not believe the truth, but took pleasure in wickedness.

Mere tolerance of the truth or respect for the truth is not enough. God is the God of truth. Anything that is feigned, phony, or an affectation is a lie. It is far better that we bear the suffering of knowing our true condition than to live deceived and deceptive lives before God and man.

Are we willing to bring to the cross all that is natural, all that we have and are, for His total correction? If we do not have the cross as the plumb line, the reality against which our own lives should be squared, how then are we assured of being built straight and true in Him? How many of us talk about the cross, but in our hearts desire that He should come down from it? Can the veil of unreality that keeps us from the glories of God and His kingdom be rent until we "give up the ghost" and cry out with a loud voice?

The crucifixion of Jesus, the ending in shameful nakedness a life that also began in nakedness, is the complete negation of every kind of conventional wisdom and religious notion that mankind could imagine. By the total negation of *all* of our life, and in the yielding up of our spirits, we enter into His glory and resurrection life. His life can only be manifested through those who have been joined with Him in death and burial, who have been raised with Him into that newness of life. God will only bury that which is dead. We will know that we have entered into death when we see evidence of the glory of the resurrection life in our own lives.

The overwhelming majority of God's people put confidence in their flesh and in their own natural ability and aptitude to live the Christian life. We may make an impressive show of it, but it is not *newness* of life. Newness, the life of God, is an utterly supernatural reality. He gives it to the destitute, the poor in spirit. We are either in that life or we are not. God has made it absolute. Where is the consistent evidence of that life in our lives?

> For you have died and your life is hidden with Christ in God. When Christ, who is our life, is revealed, then you also will be revealed with Him in glory.[58]

---

[58] Colossians 3:3-4

Are we willing to have our lives predicated on that basis? Are we willing to cease from our own efforts and the strength of our own natural ability? Our life is dead except His life be revealed, which means we will be left humiliated *often*. His glory is the glory of His life, but only when He reveals it. When *His* life will be expressed by speaking, then we speak. Trusting for His life, moment by moment, is the faith the saints of old lived by and for which they contended.

Despite the tens of thousands of bumper stickers, gospel rallies, evangelistic campaigns and other kinds of "no fuss" evangelism, the world remains largely unmoved by our Christian witness. "You shall be My witnesses"[59] is a witness that can only be given by those who have been crucified with Christ on the cross of Christ. Only then can the ultimate revelation of the truth of God be shown forth to a lost mankind through such as these.

---

[59] See Acts 1:8

CHAPTER 6

The Cross and the Triune God

T. Austin-Sparks[60] wrote that the crucifixion of Jesus had to do with God's eternal purpose, with the all-comprehending center of the universe, the hub of all truth, the basis, the issue, the explanation of everything. In other words, in the cross of Christ, God made a demonstration and a statement that would be valid through every subsequent generation. He gave the key and the clue to Himself, to His way, and to what He calls His creation to be.

We can have sympathy for a man who is crucified, but what shall we say if it is God who allows Himself to suffer at the hands of men in so unspeakable a torment and indignity? It was *God* who was crucified. When a righteous, sinless Man suffers the sin of all mankind, bearing it nobly and magnanimously, even while being mocked by His own people, then we have an ultimate revelation of not just who Jesus is, but of very God Himself. If we want to know who and what God is in His essence, look no further than what He willingly bore on the cross.

---

[60] Theodore Austin-Sparks, British Bible Commentator (1888-1971)

At the cross, more than in any other place, God is revealed as Triune. It was there that Jesus, through the eternal Spirit, offered Himself without blemish to God.[61] If we do not see God as—and in—three Persons, we lose a crucial understanding of God's very essence and being. The crucifixion of Jesus reveals all three persons of the trinity. The practical meaning and significance for us is the same as it was for Jesus: namely, we face the cross of sacrifice *through* the eternal Spirit. In the suffering of Jesus unto death, the very nature of the Holy Spirit was revealed and made manifest.

The Spirit is released to find expression and perform His work in a person wherever there is a willingness to relinquish their own ability to act using the strength inherent in their own natural humanity—that is, the flesh. This waiting upon the Spirit's work through relinquishing a dependence upon natural strength is what Jesus demonstrated in His obedient submission, suffering, and death. If Jesus endured the cross and conquered sin based upon some sort of degree of extraordinary, superhuman courage, we could admire Him, but never hope to emulate Him. But since the life and death of Jesus was predicated on the life of God—that is, because He did what He did only through the principle of complete dependence upon the eternal Spirit—we also have hope on that very same basis. We too can live "by the Spirit" because we too can relinquish our own human strength and depend utterly upon the eternal Spirit. Yet how often do we profess to believe in the triune God, and subscribe to the correctness of various doctrines, but in the actual conduct of our lives betray that which we purport to believe? In other words, we do not live and act as if we

---

[61] See Hebrews 9:14

have been brought into God's revelation of Himself in the Father, Son, and Holy Spirit.

In the Garden of Gethsemane, Jesus prayed, "Father, if You are willing, remove this cup from Me; yet not My will, but Yours be done."[62] As a Son, He was submitted to the Father in reverential deference. God exhibited that reality in Himself at great cost to Himself, a cost which involved unspeakable sufferings and death. Submission is painful. Self-will and independence are the ways the flesh wants to go. Will we ever be able to submit one to another with a true heart if we have not seen and understood the model given to us in the revelation of the Son's submission to the Father? In revealing His very essence, God gives His very being. One of the great benefits for the church is the example of the Godhead deferring one to another in gracious submission in which the One does not impose His will upon the Other. The Father exalts the Son and gives to the Son a name above every name, both in heaven and in earth. This would seem to depreciate the Father's own place; but the Father's nature is to defer and to give.

The Son does not speak His own words, nor perform His own acts; but what He hears and sees from the Father, that He does. As a Son, He lives exclusively for the glory of the Father. At the age of twelve, He confounded the doctors of the law, yet in His entire life and ministry He never acted out of His sublime humanity. Jesus is the quintessential Son. How then shall we know what true sonship is unless we understand the example of Jesus? He presented to mankind, for all time, a self-deferring Son who lived for His Father's honor. Jesus brought Himself to the cross

---

[62] Luke 22:42

to serve the Father's purposes. He trusted that the Father would raise Him from the dead. He purposed that He would not be a factor in His own resurrection from death. Everything was performed in submission to the Father. By deferring one to another, and submitting one to another as believers, we too can present to others the triune aspect of God: "That they may all be one; even as You, Father, are in Me and I in You, that they also may be in Us, so that the world may believe that You sent Me."[63]

In like manner, the Holy Spirit does not draw attention to Himself, but lives and serves to bring glory, acknowledgement, and understanding of the Son who, in turn, reveals the Father. This is the mystery of the Godhead in three Persons and the statement of who and what God is in Himself.

God is meek and lowly and humble of heart. Humility is what He is in His essential being. The Creator allowed Himself to be crucified at the hands of those He had created, thereby contradicting mankind's every definition and category of what they suppose God to be. However, God's love for mankind is such that He would not have them to live on what *they* suppose Him to be. To counter such error, He demonstrates what He is in Himself; and at the center of that demonstration is the cross of the Son. The cross demonstrates the humility of God, a God willing to suffer painful judgment and death on behalf of mankind. Undergoing the mocking, the mental trauma, the physical excruciation, nakedness and abandonment, are all a profound statement of what God is in a way that we never could have conceived or considered Him. As

---

[63] John 17:21

powerful and as glorious as He is, it is His humility that He most wants to shine forth.

Moltmann wrote that God is not greater than He is in His humiliation. He is not more glorious than He is in this self-surrender. He is not more powerful than He is in this helplessness. He is not more divine than He is in this humanity. In other words, in this self-emptying of Jesus giving Himself over in behalf of others in utter humiliation unto death, we are seeing the supreme act of love. Wherever the same self-emptying in humiliation is re-enacted in the life of the church, or of an individual believer, it is precisely there that the love of God goes forth. Wherever that kind of self-sacrifice is exhibited, God is being revealed in His essential character.

Any fellowship of believers that does not corporately reflect God in His humility is not an accurate expression of God Himself, and therefore is not the church that God intended it to be. It is through the agency of the church that God intends the revelation of Himself to be demonstrated. But we falsely represent God when we do not act or live in the central disposition of God Himself, which is His humility.

The powers of darkness dread any true exhibition of God. They yawn at the church's militant statements about "taking cities" for Christ, the mega conferences, the emphasis on demonstrations of ostensible "power", and the celebration of charismatic personalities. Only the re-enactment of the humility of God, as exhibited at the cross, terrifies the powers of darkness; it sets forth God *as God*, and they are required to flee.

Jesus disarmed and triumphed over the powers by what He demonstrated at the cross.[64] In a very real sense, so too can we, by living the cruciform life. Our

---

[64] See Colossians 2:15

inner life should be a re-enactment of the glory of what was first consummated at the cross. We inwardly experience and suffer the same convulsions that Jesus suffered. We bear, in the same humility and uncomplaining self-surrender, the mocking and insults of others. This is the majesty and glory of what the church is called to. That is why all of God's dealings with us, day after day, are designed to bring us to that place. Every time we have a difference of opinion, or some episode arises and tension results, it becomes the issue of the cross in how we respond or react. Our willingness to bear with humility and patience whatever is put before us re-enacts that same sacrifice made by Jesus.

The awareness of our own nothingness along with our willingness to experience the suffering of humiliation are necessary conditions for the releasing of His life. Those who see no need for a suffering that precedes the glory will find themselves looking for other forms of Christian life and activity, none of which can ever be a glory to God.

Moltmann writes that it is not enough for anyone to know God in His glory and His majesty without knowing Him in the lowliness and shame of the cross; that true theology and true knowledge of God lie in the *crucified* Christ; that a natural knowledge of God is potentially available to mankind, but mankind will always misuse that knowledge in the interest of their self-exaltation. He is saying that there is a way in which we can come to a sense of God from natural reason, but which does not reveal God in a way that He would have Himself to be known. We can have some valid things to say *about* God, but it will always exalt the man who has that knowledge. Only the knowledge of God that comes from the revelation given at the cross by the Holy Spirit humbles man by bringing him to the place of the truth about himself.

Within Christendom, a very real antagonism exists between those who have formed a knowledge of God from natural reason and those who have derived a knowledge of God from the crucified and resurrected Christ. Though the former may acknowledge the centrality of the cross, their real view of God is taken from a general sense of knowledge *about* Him. They are left with an inadequate view of the condition of man, and it is reflected in the way their own self-life is given pre-eminence. They *prefer* a view of God that does not call them to shame and humiliation. In the first chapter of Romans there is a profound statement warning of the dangers of knowing God from nature and natural reason. Man will celebrate the natural and created thing above the Creator Himself. To counter that, God, in His mercy, gave a revelation of Himself at the cross to save us from such a distortion.

The key statement that made Stephen's audience rush upon him to take his life was, "Behold, I see the heavens opened up and the Son of Man standing at the right hand of God."[65] The idea that a wounded, crucified man is in the eternal presence of God, at His very throne, was categorically opposed to everything his audience understood God to be. It was too devastating a blow for those who wanted to celebrate God as a distant, lofty power, far removed from the sufferings of man. How can a holy, righteous, loving and merciful God have anything to do with something as shameful as the cross? It would seem to contradict everything that human reasoning can conceive about the character of God. A crucified man standing at the right hand of God

---

[65] Acts 7:56

challenged their every religious concept. Their religious system was predicated on *their* view of God. Make no mistake: one's view of God is not some abstract thing! It affects every practicality, every action we take in our lives, every method or means whereby we express ourselves and relate to others. When Stephen's statement conflicted with their view of God, they ventilated their antagonism upon him by killing him.

The true church can realistically expect to suffer at the hands of those who have a self-serving view of God. They will react in similar manner, either with words, or with force, in order to remove anyone who makes God known in truth. They will kill and claim they are doing God a service; but to what "God" are they doing a service? It is the god of their own imagining. When those who see the heavens opened reveal the truth of God to them, the foundation of their reality is challenged, threatened and revealed as false.

Can you imagine the stones that hit Stephen thudding against *your* body? How do we presently react when someone gives us an indifferent look, or fails to give us the acknowledgement we feel is due us? Can we bear it, or does our flesh clamor in protest? Stephen felt those stones breaking flesh and bone. He was slowly battered to death, but he never reacted in kind against his murderers. In the depth of his suffering, in the bearing of it, he revealed the gracious magnanimity of God. He patiently surrendered to it, and in his resignation we have a profound revelation of the character of God. It is not a masochistic suffering, but a suffering as God bears it, thereby showing what God's heart is. It is to this same redemptive suffering that the church is called as the only means by which God so profoundly reveals Himself to mankind.

No man is capable of that kind of magnanimity unless his life has been transformed by the sacrificial Lamb Himself. Though Saul may not have been physically present at the crucifixion of Jesus, he saw in Stephen's death the very re-enactment of that event *for his sake*. Though he may not have understood it with his mind, as brilliant as he was, the reality and the power of it were irrefutable. The god of his own pharisaical imagining met the God who revealed Himself at the cross. On the road to Damascus, this revelation finally struck him in the words of the resurrected and ascended Christ: "Saul, Saul, why are you persecuting Me?"[66]

Stephen's martyrdom contains profound, timeless elements that are re-enacted in every true martyrdom. His statement before his audience was not something calculated to please or pacify them. They were already calling him a blasphemer, so he knew that he was in a place of danger. Instead of speaking soothing, carefully selected thoughts that would ease their displeasure, he seemed to have almost intentionally rubbed them the wrong way. He recounted the history of Israel's consistent apostasy and failure from Moses onwards. He then added, "You men who are stiff-necked and uncircumcised in heart and ears are always resisting the Holy Spirit; you are doing just as your fathers did."[67] He spoke of an unbroken continuum: that they were one with their fathers and, in fact, they soon proved his point by killing him as their fathers killed the prophets.

Stephen was a man beneath Saul's dignity, a waiter on tables, while Saul was the prized student of the rabbi Gamaliel. The gracious way in which Stephen suffered and died would have struck Saul's heart. Stephen's last

---

[66] Acts 9:4b
[67] Acts 7:51

words, "Lord, do not hold this sin against them!"[68] were a revelation of a reality beyond the categories of religion: namely, a revelation of very God Himself. Stephen re-enacted the cross in his willing suffering for another by bearing the agony without retaliating in kind.

In a very real sense, the baptism of Jesus was a depiction of the cross. His going down into the Jordan River as the Son of Man, to fulfill all righteousness, was a statement to the Father and to the powers of darkness: "I am commencing My ministry as the Son of God, but it is not going to be predicated on My natural ability and gifting. Though I am the supreme Son of Man, and can make an impressive show of it on that basis, I am going down into a death, dying to My own natural humanity. I will never seek to serve the Father on the basis of what is in man." When He came up from that "death," the Spirit of God came upon Him as the source and the statement of His life and being.

With the Spirit comes the revelation of God in His essential being. Jesus was then driven by the Spirit into the wilderness for a forty-day trial of self-denial and temptation to come off from that ground. Jesus' life and ministry began with the cross and then ended with that very same cross. His every act was an act of self-denial, a cross-enactment. In other words, Jesus lived in the spirit of self-sacrifice and crucifixion before he tasted the actual event of crucifixion. We are called to exactly the same reality: namely, to deny our self-life a pre-eminence, to bear insult, injury, rejection. We are called to a cruciform lifestyle in every aspect of our life and being.

The world is cross-avoiding. The cross-centered life challenges everything that the world values and

---

[68] See Acts 7:60b

upholds. It may have its religious forms, its political, social, and economic forms, but they are all opposed to the truth of God. Wherever those are touched by cross-centeredness, we will see indignation, anger, and bitterness rise up against it. The spirit of antichrist will always react to any threat against its vested self-interests. The antichrist spirit is not just a general rejection of Christ; it is the specific rejection of the *crucified* Christ. It may insist on a God who it wants to call "Christ", but is not the *suffering* Christ. It celebrates an imagined figure more in keeping with what it thinks a lofty God ought to be. The antichrist spirit despises the shame of the cross, though it will employ the word "cross" in its vocabulary. At heart, it is a spirit that substitutes for the true God its own false image of God.

Where the reality of the cross is resonant in any believer, mankind arches its back, sensing that what is represented in that person is antithetical and contrary to everything upon which their false reality is predicated. The last days will reveal these oppositions more acutely. It will be critical in these days for true believers to know why they are opposed and be steadfast in cleaving to the cross of Christ, because only what is represented in *that* cleaving has the power to set men free. The world needs to be set free from its delusions and a phony church needs to be set free from its deceptions. Only the truth and reality of God as set forth in the suffering of God, as revealed at the cross of God, has the power to do that.

Everything about the cross of Christ is abhorrent to human sensibility. It is as if God went out of His way, knowing man and his disposition, to set forth something calculated to offend his every category and to say, "If you reject this, you reject any knowledge of Me." We have paid deeply for our rejection. It has left us with a distorted view, not only of the knowledge of God, but of the presence of God. If the crucifixion of Jesus cost the Father unbelievable pain, how must He regard our sinful rejection of it? And what are the consequences of that rejection for us?

Most of us desire a form of God and a form of godliness in which we adhere to and teach correct biblical principles *about* God and the faith—especially when we think they are derived from His word. It is comforting for the flesh to have a God who allows us a certain form of religious self-respect. Men draw away from a God who is Lord over all, who requires the death of our natural self, who has a standard of holiness. God saves men from their own inadequate concepts of Him and from fashioning Him in *their* image of how they would like Him to be, which will always serve *their* purposes. God calls that idolatry, but He saves mankind from it by calling them back to the cross and to the "shock" of what the cross represents. Idolatry gives men the form of religion while it allows them to continue as lords of their own lives, making their own determinations. To contend for the faith is in essence to keep the issue of the cross alive in the meaning God gave it rather than allowing its meaning to dissipate away.

Chapter 7

The Cross and Preaching the Gospel

Paul could say that he preached "Christ crucified."[69] To some degree, we all are called to be preachers; called to be witnesses, called to share. Therefore we ought to know what "preaching Christ crucified" means before we open our mouths for God. This kind of preaching is scarce, which is an unhappy statement of the absence of the work of the cross in the lives of many of God's people. We cannot call our hearers to a reality that we have not ourselves first attained and consistently maintain.

One man will speak a message that leaves us totally unaffected and unchallenged; but another, speaking almost the same message, leaves us trembling and compels us to decide for or against God. The word that truly preaches Christ crucified has the power to create faith in the hearing; it becomes an event, a word that performs a work. Many preachers are content to preach a correct sermon rather than a sermon as "event" because the cross is not yet central in the reality of their own lives. They have themselves not yet come to the cross in truth. The sermon may be biblically correct, but

---

[69] See 1 Corinthians 1:23

it can never be a call to the cross until the reality of the cross has been worked into the preacher's life.

One wonders what Isaiah saw when he cried out, "Woe is me, for I am ruined!"[70] Did he perhaps catch some glimpse of the crucified Christ, a prefiguring of what was yet to come? He saw something that devastated his knowledge of what he thought he knew about God. To see God *as God* is to be undone and ruined *as man*. It is to be struck with the fear of God, the awe of God. It came to him as a vision; and it came *before* God sent him. God will not send anyone who has not first come to this place of seeing. The same could be said of Moses when he killed the Egyptian. Though he was the right man to deliver Israel, he had not yet come to a right understanding of himself. His was a human zeal. He looked this way and that, but he did not look up. It took forty more years to be emptied of himself before the revelation of God came to him in the burning bush.

When a true word is preached, whatever the subject matter, it is a call to the cross. It makes a requirement of the hearers, bringing them to the recognition of the necessity to make the cross *central* to their lives. All too many of us have been satisfied with merely correct sermons that require nothing from us other than a nod of our heads. The issue of salvation depends on the preaching of a crucified Christ. Paul writes: "How then will they call on Him in whom they have not believed? How will they believe in Him whom they have not heard?"[71] We have heard many sermons *about* Christ, but have we heard Christ set forth as crucified in the power of God? This is another kind of speaking, one that leaves the hearer without excuse as to who God is.

---

[70] Isaiah 1:5
[71] Romans 10:14a

When received, it births faith to believe, for "faith comes from hearing, and hearing by the word of Christ,"[72] which is different from the word of man. The word of man may be biblically sound and doctrinally correct, but that does not make it, for that reason, the word of God. A word *about* Christ is not the same as the word *of* Christ.

The cross is at the center of the reality of the true preached word. To rightly preach the word requires from the preacher a radical dependency upon God. Having sought the Lord and prepared himself, he abandons himself to the life of God, knowing that there might be every possibility of a humiliating failure. This is where the cross really becomes the cross. Every true preaching is the reiteration of the cross in the life of the preacher, but only when self-abandonment, itself an act of suffering, prevails in the speaker. If we are unwilling to risk self-abandonment, if we are fearful of disappointing our hearers, or if we fear men more than we fear God, we circumvent the cross. Even though our subject matter might actually be *about* the cross, it is not necessarily a "cross" message.

When we preach the word, the cross does not have to be the explicit subject matter. Jesus was His message. You cannot say where the word ended and the Man began, or where the word began and the Man ended. The Man was the word: "In the beginning was the Word, and the Word was with God, and the Word was God."[73] To a very real degree, it could also be said that Paul himself was the message. The cross was implicit in all that issued from his apostolic life, because his apostolic life was itself centered in the cross.

---

[72] Ibid., v.17
[73] John 1:1

In the spoken word, God's name and honor are at stake. If a "Christ and Him crucified" word is going forth, then God is being communicated in His essential being. The word sets forth God as He in fact is. He is always set forth in resurrection power and life wherever there is a death that precedes that resurrection. The greatest anguish of soul on the part of the preacher is when God does not seem to come through *as God*, when He has seemingly abandoned him. It may well be that the bearing of that humiliation is *exactly* what God wants communicated. God abandoned His own Son at the most excruciating and significant moment, leaving the Son to cry out, "My God, My God, why have You forsaken me!" That is the *real* death—that sense of being abandoned or forsaken. It was the frequent anguish of the psalmists, "O God, how long are You going to allow Yourself to be scorned? I am not seeking to be alleviated from their harassment, but I want to see You set forth as God." The psalmists could bear their personal suffering, but they agonized over the loss to God's name. While God was not answering, His enemies poured contempt upon Him. It is God's sovereign prerogative to seemingly forsake His own. It is His freedom as God to either assert Himself or to withdraw Himself in the fulfillment of His own purpose and will. We have to allow God to be God, even, or maybe especially, when He is ostensibly absent.

The cross was a symbol of weakness, of total impotence, of a God who seemingly could not save Himself. The cross signified total humiliation and degradation. This is the both the glory and the scandal of the message of the cross. Of what shall we be proud if God Himself suffered this indignity? And did He not suffer it to meet the issue of *our* pride, so that we would not have any grounds to keep ourselves from the kinds of things that would be a humiliation for us? If He willingly suffered ultimate humiliation, we who claim to be led by the Spirit should also be as willing.

To preach the gospel of Christ is to preach Christ crucified. If men have any consideration for God at all, they will always conceive of some lofty image appropriate to the dignity of what they think deity should be. But a crucified God has no dignity. Crucifixion is contrary to anything one would think God ought to experience; but the cross is God's wisdom because it reveals Him in truth, as He truly is.

> For I am not ashamed of the gospel, for it is the power of God for salvation to everyone who believes, to the Jew first and also to the Greek. For in it the righteousness of God is revealed from faith to faith; as it is written, "BUT THE RIGHTEOUS *man* SHALL LIVE BY FAITH."[74]

The apostle has to disarm any disposition to be embarrassed by the gospel message by saying that he himself is not ashamed. Paul knew that his proclamation had an inherent power unto salvation to everyone who would cleave to the truth of its revelation of God. There ought to be nothing we need to be ashamed of because we know what it saves humanity from. However, if we do not understand or apprehend the exceeding sinfulness of sin in which every human soul abides, then we *will* be ashamed, and we will find ourselves preaching only correct principles related to the faith rather than the truth of the gospel itself.

How, then, is the righteousness of God revealed in the gospel? How is the gospel the most acute and profound statement of God's righteousness? The gospel is essentially God's provision to achieve the

---

[74] Romans 1:16-17

reconciliation of a lost mankind back to Himself through the shedding of blood by His Son as both perfect man and God. No lesser sacrifice would have or could have sufficed. All previous animal sacrifices and atonement for sin were in anticipation of what God would provide *in Himself* as the once-and-for-all sacrifice. God, who is rightly angry at sin, paid the price that justice required in order to expiate sin, or else He would not have been a righteous God.

Jesus revealed the righteousness of God in voluntarily bearing the cross. The sufferings of Jesus unto death depicted that righteousness. Righteousness will not let sin pass without an appropriate response. How would God be righteous if He turned a blind eye toward sin? God expresses His righteous indignation at what sin is, because sin, in the last analysis, is a direct affront to God. It is a willful attitude and conduct on the part of man against God. It is a posture of disrespect and contempt in the light of God's requirement, "Thou shall not..."

If we do not have any real consciousness of the exceeding sinfulness of sin, we will not see the necessity for the *expiation* of our own sin. We presume upon God when we seek to obtain forgiveness for our sin without realizing the need to see our sin expiated. We must understand sin and why God is angry with the sinner every day—"God is a righteous judge, and a God who has indignation every day."[75] "The boastful shall not stand before Your eyes; You hate all who do iniquity."[76]

We have no message for a dying world until we ourselves have understood the magnitude of our own sin. If David, the King of Israel, a man "after God's

---

[75] Psalm 7:11
[76] Psalm 5:5

own heart", and the author of many psalms, could fall into adultery and murder, make no mistake—we are all capable of that very same conduct. Why are our sins not "ever before us," like David's were? Must we commit those same sins to reveal that we share with David the same essential Adamic (i.e. sinful) nature?

In Jesus' entire earthly ministry, the only work that He acknowledged as being good was Mary's breaking of the alabaster vial of perfume. About this He said, "Truly I say to you, wherever this gospel is preached in the whole world, what this woman has done will also be spoken of in memory of her."[77] Mary's act of devotion was completely in keeping with the gospel itself; it was a sacrifice of extravagant outpouring. Jesus poured out His life; she poured out an expensive fragrance.

Many of us are doctrinally correct, but we lack an outpouring of the fragrance of God, and, because of that, God's house lacks the fragrance of the knowledge of Him. The only way to pour out the fragrance of God from our own alabaster lives is by our own breaking. However, our breaking is relative to our understanding of the magnitude of what has been poured out for us by the Lord Himself (those who have been forgiven much love much). It was a remarkable act by Mary; but it evoked an indignant response from the disciples; they saw her act as an unnecessary waste. God poured Himself out lavishly at the cross. He sent His own Son to earth, taking on the form of a man, being confined in an earthly body. He suffered the humiliation of that restriction and limitation, as a son of Abraham, the despised race. Then He suffered a death of the most scandalous kind. Can God the Father be more lavish than that?

---

[77] Matthew 26:13

How many of us have seen people convicted by *our* proclamation of the gospel? Do we give an explanation of the gospel in humanly, rational terms that lessen its impact, robbing it completely of its power? Are we guilty of packaging the gospel to make it more acceptable to our hearers? Can we proclaim the gospel with conviction and authority? Or is it just a helpful suggestion, a casual option we offer to those we consider "lost". Do we frame the gospel as piercing, unavoidable truth—or as merely our own opinion?

In the rest of Romans chapter 1, Paul outlines the consequences of unbelief in rejecting the gospel. Mankind everywhere has forsaken the clear evidence of God as Creator. God's righteous wrath reveals itself, and will reveal itself, against man's forsaking such clear and compelling evidence. His anger is not the human petulance that we so often exhibit. God's wrath is the right and just response of a holy God to mankind's turning away from Him in their hearts, thoughts, and conduct. This is especially so when they have had every reason to acknowledge and know God in His creation. Paul says that we are *all* without excuse.

How many missionaries, laboring in far-away countries and cultures, really believe the testimony of Paul that *all everywhere* are without excuse? Those who live in primitive savagery are, as well as those living in civilized luxury, without excuse. They both reveal they are under judgment. They are thoroughly cursed in their sin. Their minds are obdurate, their hearts are darkened. In the jungles of Africa or the jungles of New York, men can murder and pillage without any compunction because they have already forfeited the revelation of God through creation. Their condition, and especially their ingratitude toward each other, is a statement of that judgment.

Missionaries need to know that they are not coming to a primitive people who need to evolve from pagan primitivism to the acknowledgment of a monotheistic God, and then to the more sophisticated recognition of the gospel and revelation of Jesus, unto discipleship. Primitive savagery, the disregard for human life, the base degeneration inherent in many aspects of their lives, is a statement that they are already under judgment. Many missionaries come back broken and burned out from their failure to reach the lost, because they have not realized the people to whom they were ministering are facing a judgment for the forfeiture of God—and such judgment is not something from which they can "evolve" toward salvation. Those to whom we come must instead be confronted and accused with the fact that their condition is the very statement of their sin.

When men like Jonathan Edwards or Charles Finney preached, their hearers were known to clutch at the pews and pillars of the church building lest they slip through the floor and into the fires of hell itself, which heat they felt in the soles of their feet by the very preaching. It was called "hellfire and brimstone" preaching. But what has happened to that kind of preaching in modern times? It is almost as if such messages are now obsolete or ridiculed into obscurity, and we have "graduated" to more elevated forms of the gospel message. Yet the truth remains that the most powerful and effective messages first persuade people that they are sinners. Unless men see their condition and repent, they will surely perish. Jesus Himself said, "Unless you believe that I am He, you will die in your sins."[78] There is no second chance once you descend into hell. It is an eternal and irremediable fate, an unbroken anguish of soul…but it is also a just penalty

---

[78] John 8:24b

because the wages of our sin is death.

How much time have we spent in books and libraries chasing after knowledge about a subject in order to fulfill the requirements of a degree so that we will have a route to financial security and success? In comparison, how much time have we spent examining the words of the Man who purported to be the Messiah of Israel and very God Himself, who had come to earth, at a certain point in time, to effect a redemption, for the rejection of which there will be an eternal penalty? How much time have we spent considering eternity itself? How much time have we spent considering God Himself? We will be judged for what we have chosen to ignore. We need to bring the whole counsel of God to bear upon mankind. They need to know that their unbelieving is willful. They are already suffering the consequence of their unbelief, which is godlessness and unrighteousness. If the penalty for such unbelief in this life is bad, what shall we say about the penalty of the Hell to come?

When we willfully reject the truth of God for a lie, God gives us over to degrading passions. Paul cites women exchanging their natural function for that which is not natural, a perverse and degrading passion for each other.[79] When a woman gives over the natural function of her body, it is a statement that she is under the judgment of God for forfeiting the righteousness of God. The same principle applies to men.[80] In other words, homosexuality is the *consequence* of willful acts of disbelief and rebellion; homosexuality is a judgment for sins already performed in rejecting the righteous God. Like every other painful result of every other sin we commit, the condition of homosexuality is judgment—

---

[79] Romans 1:26
[80] Ibid., v.27

and the judgment itself is God's provision to bring that person to a place of repentance. And as we would for every other sinner, they need to be told in a way that does not exalt us at their expense. They need to see the wickedness of their condition, that there is no escape and no remedy except through the power of the gospel.

Being an apostle of God, Paul speaks the truth of God. We need to submit to that truth, or else we will be tempted to go along and say, "Oh, the poor victims. They couldn't help it. It must be something genetic." Homosexuality and lesbianism are not caused by some genetic defect, but these lifestyles are deliberately and voluntarily chosen; they are choices for which those who practice these sins will be held accountable and pay the penalty, both in this life and the life to come. They have allowed themselves to give over the natural function of their own bodies—a sign that God has abandoned them to their illicit lust. Perverse immorality is necessarily the logical outworking of that abandonment. The sin itself is the rejection of God *as God*. That is what all sin is. They are without excuse; they have ignored the testimony of creation and the testimony of God's word, and now they are suffering the consequence of a willful ignorance. The word of God is the defining statement of truth. No immoral person need ever think he can enter the kingdom of God.[81]

Have you noticed how much the gospel is being denigrated and diluted in our contemporary Christendom? Rather than a call to radical separation unto God, today's gospel message is one of improvement and of how to enjoy that improvement. This culturally adaptive gospel does not confront us with a condition that requires a union with the Crucified One

---

[81] See Revelation 21:8

in death, burial, and resurrection to a newness of life. To paraphrase scripture, "As its ministers, so also the church, and as the church, so also the nation." The church is fully accountable for the moral condition of its nation. Paul ends his statement with:

> Although they know the ordinance of God, that those who practice such things are worthy of death, they not only do the same, but also give hearty approval to those who practice them.[82]

The grace of God has given a rudimentary benefit to mankind called conscience, but our consciences can be seared[83] and deadened by continually disregarding its insistent voice. Mankind rejects God because it does not want a God of righteousness and law to tell them what to do. We do not want to be infringed upon. We want to do our own thing as if we ourselves are God.

The final outworking of sin is when we approve of evil as being somehow good. We pervert truth so as to believe that black is white, that wrong is right. When we willfully reject the knowledge of God, we are abandoned to the outworking of our own lusts in their most degrading forms. Whatever man sows, that shall he reap. This is a moral law in the universe that needs to be recognized, and we see it being acted out in our day, no matter how loudly the world tries to shout it into oblivion. This is an evil age, but do we hate or speak out against its iniquity?

To be a witness for God requires a union with His death. Only the cross upon which Jesus was impaled can do that. If we shrink from that union with His death, we are not in a place to proclaim the gospel. Are we ashamed of the gospel? How do we react when it comes

---

[82] Romans 1:32
[83] See Ephesians 4:19

to the nitty-gritty of speaking to a respectable person whose life is morally, culturally, and intellectually more impressive than ours? Can we bring ourselves to communicate this message, which most will consider foolishness, or will we shrink back?

Have we made our peace with a righteous God who has established a hell in which there is an eternal burning without remedy, where souls writhe in an anguish that can never be comforted? Are we reconciled to a God who is not only a God of heaven, but also of hell? Are we wondering why God could not find a way for human redemption without the necessity of that threat? Or do we realize that righteousness itself requires a literal hell? Hell is a just and righteous recompense for a life lived indifferently to God. Hell is not at all an offense to God, but is totally in keeping with what He is in Himself as righteous. We like God's mercy, His love and His kindness, but do we equally love His judgments and Himself as judge?

> He has fixed a day in which He will judge the world in righteousness through a Man whom He has appointed, having furnished proof to all men by raising Him from the dead.[84]

By appointing a specific Man to judge the world, God establishes a Judge whom we all will face. And when we stand before that man, He will have scars that remind us that He is fit to judge because He has suffered and paid the full price of judgment in being Himself judged. What excuse will we give then? What justification will we have for our willful sin against God and our failure to heed and regard Him, though He has made many efforts to speak to us? What will we say to Him in that Day when we, in this day, have so

---

[84] Acts 17:31

obstinately disregarded His warnings? The Day of Judgment is a fearful thing to contemplate.

"Repent and believe in the gospel."[85] It is only through repentance that faith comes. Repentance is the key to believing. If we are hardened and unrepentant, we will never come into the true knowledge of God. Any sharing of the gospel must be from the place of our own brokenness and sense of our nothingness before God. Only then can we rightly speak a word that challenges a person to repentance. We are equally guilty of every sin. Grace and mercy came to us totally undeserved in order that we should move others to jealousy by the gracious exhibition of what we have obtained.

Until we bring the gospel to the Jew, we do not know how foolish the gospel really is. What Jews represent in themselves will constantly remind us of the absurdity of the message we are called to proclaim. In their dignity, prestige and celebration of themselves as a moral and ethical people, they are the antithesis of that foolishness. Someone once said that nothing more reveals the radical content of the gospel than its confrontation with the synagogue. God insists we take the gospel "to the Jew first"[86] to rub our faces into this contradiction. We are to begin with the very people who crucified Him and stoned His prophets. Once we can weather *that* storm, so to speak, by the power of the message itself, then can we rightly go to the Gentiles. Many of us have ignored that priority, as if God has not spoken through Paul to the church.

The gospel can bring mankind to the true knowledge of God because there is an intrinsic power in

---

85 Mark 1:15b
86 See Romans 1:16

the message of the gospel to do that work. Are we willing to trust for that even at the risk of our embarrassment? If we will not face that possibility, how do we go on to anything in God in the realm of faith if we miss it here at the first? That is why Paul speaks about the gospel at the beginning of his letter, not just for our academic contemplation, but also for our obedience.

The cross calls us to suffer the indignation of those to whom we witness. In His witness to mankind, Jesus Himself suffered total degradation and naked humiliation before His own people. Therefore, we are without excuse if we shrink from our much lesser humiliation in view of that which He voluntarily shouldered. Because He bore it, and was willing to be brought down in that humiliation, God exalted Him and gave Him a name above every name both in heaven and earth, and a throne higher than the heavens. God exalts those who are willing to be humbled. Our eternal place and reward are altogether proportionate to the humiliations we are willing to bear in this life in obedience to God. Jesus Himself is evidence that He who was abased is now exalted. Likewise, our willingness to suffer humiliation takes on new meaning when seen in light of the exaltation that will be ours eternally in heaven.

CHAPTER 8

The Cross and Water Baptism

Apparently the believers in Rome had submitted themselves to water baptism without knowing its spiritual significance. Therefore, Paul raised the question: "Or do you not *know* that all of us who have been baptized into Christ Jesus have been baptized into His death?"[87]

Do *we* know? Do we *want* to know? Who wants to be baptized into a death? Death is unsavory. The very word sends a chill down our spines, but the heart of the faith is predicated upon the word *death*. That is what is implied in water baptism. Of all of the forms for being baptized, total immersion is the form that most represents a burial. It is a joining with Jesus in His death through burial. Even though we may celebrate and honor the truth of the resurrection of Jesus, we will be living effectually outside of its power if we have not first joined Him in death and burial. It seems elementary to say it, but death is either total or it is not death at all. Without the totality of death, we can forget what follows: namely, the resurrection power of new life.

---

[87] Romans 6:3

How do we view our own baptism? What did it mean for us when we went into those waters? What does it mean for us now? There is a way in which we can be immersed in water without any true comprehension of what we are doing except for a sense that we have fulfilled some sort of biblical obligation. If we have not come into the existential reality of burial with Him in death, we are not going to know the power to live a heavenly life in a world that is as much at enmity with God's people as it was with the Lord Himself.

If we have not known and have not appropriated, by faith, what baptism is given for, we will not be capable of showing forth the resurrected Christ. What instead will be conveyed is testimony about ourselves, about our ability to keep the correct principles of the faith, about our moral respectability. In that lesser place, we can never exhibit and show forth the Lord. We can exhibit man at his best, which is nice, but man at his best will never be a glory to God. Only the manifestation of His life redounds to His glory.

As a response to join the Lord in death and burial, baptism ends not just our embarrassing carnality but also the totality of our Adamic nature in its most respectable forms. God says that nothing good dwells in our human flesh.[88] When are we going to agree with Him? When are we going to recognize that striving to do well out of our own nature, our own humanity, however much it may please us and our neighbor, falls short of the glory of God? Even our best is not good enough. It is still *our* natural humanity, filled with sin and ego, vanity, and pride. It can never serve God in a priestly way, for

---

[88] Romans 7:18

as long as the root of self remains, there will always be a self-serving element.

Death is the key to life. The bringing forth of life out of death is more than merely resuscitating the old; it is ushering in a new dimension of being, a radical re-orientation of life and purpose. Are we willing to relinquish the basis and foundation of our own natural life and ability in order to obtain His life? However gifted we may be in the natural, are we willing to cast ourselves, in faith, upon the hope of another life?

To put it another way, are we willing to bring to death our religious success, the best of what we are, trusting that another life will transform ours? Is there in us a desire to live increasingly free from the taint of self-seeking, self-interest, and everything that disfigures the lives of those who are still alive to themselves? Have we come to the place where we have truly despaired of ourselves? Despair is a blessing. To come to the end of ourselves is a mercy from God. It is better to know that we have lived consistently beneath the level of God's glory in this life *now* than to find that out standing before God in the Day of Judgment.

The main reason why more of God's people are not driven to despair is that we do not have any desire to put to death the natural man. We shun the idea that we are no longer the determining factor in how we order our lives. We have little enthusiasm for anyone else to tell us what to do, especially an invisible God. We lack the intensity to serve God with *all* of our heart, mind, strength, and soul. We lack the willingness for our lives to be ordered by another sovereign entity, with all the uncertainty and hardships and sacrifices that are implied and required. We are a generation that wants to succeed at minimal cost. Every one of these considerations shows who is really at the center of our lives; it is the *self*, wanting to be gratified, wanting to succeed, wanting to be seen and acknowledged.

Our entrenched self-life always seeks its own ends. It cannot be rectified—that is, made right before God—by any human means. Our nauseating egotism, this sickly, sinful thing that it is, demands self-recognition, self-celebration and self-gratification. It will never let us go. In other words, we can never alter the disposition of self to seek its own ends. Who can save us from this body of self? Only God has the answer: namely, the bringing of that whole Adamic nature to the cross, to death and burial. God's answer is not to *reform* self, to correct it, or to placate it, but to put it to death. If we thought of ourselves as wicked sinners, we would rush to obtain the provision of the cross; but thinking ourselves nice guys, at least in our own eyes, we are not all that anxious!

> Therefore we have been buried with Him through baptism into death, so that as Christ was raised from the dead through the glory of the Father, so we too might walk in newness of life. For if we have become united with Him in the likeness of His death, certainly we shall also be in the likeness of His resurrection, knowing this, that our old self was crucified with Him, in order that our body of sin might be done away with, so that we would no longer be slaves to sin, for he who has died is freed from sin.[89]

"Newness of life" is true life and true being, but it can only be wrought in us and brought forth by the power of God. Finally, we can have access to a life that no longer serves itself. The self-life is put to death in order to make way for the new life—*His* Life—which

---

[89] Romans 6:4-7

will transform and have expression through us. This is what baptism means, but how many of us have understood and desired this identification?

Spiritual newness can never be forced upon us. The God who gave Himself in totality asks that we give ourselves in the same totality. By this identification and union, we rise to a newness of life. Through His own death and resurrection, God has made available to us this most profound reality.

"Even so consider yourselves to be dead to sin, but alive to God in Christ Jesus."[90] We cannot consider ourselves dead to sin and self unless we have been through a radical surrender of our will before God. We cannot employ this verse as true for us unless we have appropriated the reality it speaks of. A.W. Tozer noted that the scriptures tell us *how* to be saved and sanctified, but they cannot confirm to us that we *are* saved or sanctified. In other words, the reality has to be appropriated before the scriptures are a true statement of us.

Paul could say, "I have been crucified with Christ; and it is no longer I who live, but Christ lives in me."[91] The life of the indwelling Christ has now become his, but it came when he forfeited and counted as dung all that he had relished and celebrated in himself. Paul is the personification of the crucified man. He is the man who is saved to the uttermost, and he makes salvation rest upon the appropriation of two things:

> That if you confess with your mouth Jesus as Lord, and believe in your heart that God raised Him from the dead, you will be saved.[92]

---

[90] Romans 6:11
[91] Galatians 2:20a
[92] Romans 10:9

In other words, if we will not believe that God raised Jesus from the dead, how shall we believe that He will raise us? And we must do so not just once, but continually, as often as we consider ourselves *indeed* as dead to sin and self, but alive to God in Christ Jesus.

The powers of the air are not in the least threatened by an individual or a fellowship that still functions out of its own well-meaning strength. They are only threatened by those who are alive in God by the power of His life, whose purpose is to serve Him and to live for Him out of that power. The choice is ours. How far do we want to go in God? Are we willing for the end of our natural life, our thoughts, our intentions, our ambitions, our hopes? Are we willing then to allow His life to transform our own? Do we want our lives to count for Him before this age concludes?

The Scriptures warn us about works that will be burned up in the judgment of God; they will be as hay, wood, and stubble.[93] These will be works that have originated in our minds, conceived and acted out within the framework of our own ability and strength. However, the works that endure, the gold, silver and precious stones, are the works that have their origin in God. They are works that are beyond anything of our own natural ability to perform. They can only be performed on the basis of His life, to those who are consistently yielded, emptied, and surrendered.

When we are truly apprehended by God's remarkable statement of Himself at the cross, we are drawn to give ourselves in a union of identification with His nature. Baptism then becomes the reinforcing and declaration of our answering intent. As someone noted: "In this self-giving, Christ and the Christian become,

---

[93] See 1 Corinthians 3:12-15

and are, a single totality."[94]   In our union with Him in this totality, He truly becomes our Lord.   Outside of that union, we only maintain a religious posture by which we invoke a certain vocabulary that is not in fact true for us. He is not our Lord until He has the *totality* of our lives. And if He does not have it in baptism, He does not have it at all.

Union through baptism brings us into a quality of relationship through the very life of God that is given. Every time we come to the communion table in truth, we are nurturing and renewing the life and nature of God in us.   Without this understanding, we are doing with the bread and wine what we have already done with water baptism: namely, making of it a ceremonial, external commemoration.   It becomes only a reminder, an emblem, an act that has no inward corresponding power and value.   God is the God of truth, and we have to come to Him in truth.   Only then will the communion table convey to us the life and essence of the Lord.

Holy Communion affirms a covenant of union that we have made with God through baptism.   The eating and drinking are fresh enablement of that life to continue serving God.   One cannot serve God on the basis of well-wishing intentions, and that is why He gave us these great witnesses, the two great sacraments of water baptism and communion.   The great shame of the Protestant Church is that we have transformed both of these into mindless ceremonies.   Our inability to touch the community around us, let alone the world, is the evidence of that shame and failure.

In baptism, God has provided a sacrament, a means by which we can obtain the benefit of His death.   He is not asking us to impale ourselves on a wooden object.

---

[94] Quote unknown

There is only one death, the epochal event in all history, the crucifixion of God Himself. But we can enter into that reality and receive the benefit of it by means of baptism. In baptism, He is inviting us to identify and join Him in His very death.

If we think of baptism as only a religious requirement or obligation, then our self remains just as alive when we come out of the water as it was when we went in. Is it possible to go into the waters of baptism and to derive no more benefit from it than one who had been sprinkled as an infant? Not only is it possible, but such might actually describe most believers' baptisms. They went into it as a religious requirement without any conscious awareness that it should have been a descent into death. They had no intention of forsaking their self-life; they were just performing what they thought to be a scriptural command. Therefore, having missed it there, they are living beneath the glory of God. God has done everything, but if we do not avail ourselves of it in truth, it becomes, for us, only a religious ceremony rather than a holy sacrament.

We will not be willing for a baptism unto death unless we really despair of the natural man. As long as there is any hope to serve God by the natural man, baptism does us not one whit of good. As long as we hope to be "spiritual" in the strength of our natural man, we are not bringing anything to the waters of death; we are just bringing verbal categories into the water, and we come up the same as we went down—unchanged. It is not a going down into the Jordan of death because we still want to retain our natural life. Until we despair and agree with God that in man there is no good thing at all, we have not gone into those waters of death. Let us not be guilty of hindering the righteousness of God by adhering to correct doctrine without the existential reality of that doctrine. Let us press on to a deepened appreciation for the phenomenon of baptism. May we at last comprehend what it meant for Jesus who *was* raised from the dead, and what it would mean for us as well.

CHAPTER 9

The Cross as Foolishness

God makes choices, and if we want to understand God, we need to know what He chooses because what He chooses reveals who and what He is in Himself. We must also be aware that *our* own choices reveal who *we* really are. What we do with our time, what we do with our money, whom we select as friends, the things that we read, the things that engage us, reveal who we are. Everything that God chooses reveals who He is, and at the same time contradicts what the world celebrates and esteems. God delights in choosing the things that are weak, foolish, and despised in the eyes of the world in order to establish the holy and glorious. He wants to rub into our consciousness that the way of the kingdom is utterly contrary to the way of the world. We need to burrow in to understand why God chooses what He chooses, and to determine whether we ourselves deeply agree with those choices *and* His way of choosing. To agree with His choices means not just to nod our heads in agreement, but to live, move, and have our being in those same essential choices.

By choosing crucifixion for His Son, God the Father shattered conventional Jewish religious understanding of what it meant to relate to Moses and the Law of God., not to mention their deficient understanding of who and what the Messiah would be. Failing in the requirement to love God with all their heart, their soul, their mind, and their strength, making of God's intended relationship instead a legalistic structure of rules and regulations, they failed to recognize the God of Sinai in the man Jesus. That failure revealed there never was a love for God or knowledge of Him in the first place. They were faced with the mind-boggling conundrum of trying to rightly imagine what God was like. The crucified Figure before them completely contradicted those expectations.

The interpretation that we bring to something is invariably the statement about ourselves. How then do we understand these words of Jesus to His disciples?

> Go into the village opposite you, and immediately you will find a donkey tied there and a colt with her; untie them and bring them to Me. If anyone says anything to you, you shall say, "The Lord has need of them, and immediately he will send them."[95]

Why would Jesus need *both* animals if He only intended to ride on the back of one of them? There is as much instruction in what He chose *not* to employ as what He chose *to* employ. The wisdom of this world would say, "Don't look like an idiot jolting about on a small, unbroken animal upon which no man has ever sat. That is foolish. You're the King. You need to sit on an animal that is mature, that has carried men before, one that can be trusted." The Mount of Olives is so steep that one can barely *walk* down it and still maintain one's dignity. Imagine a full-grown man coming down that

---

[95] See Matthew 21:2-3

descent on such a small, spindly, untried animal. By every reckoning Jesus should have come down on an animal that had been prepared to bear Him, but instead He chose an animal that had never before borne anyone. He chose the shameful, embarrassing and humiliating thing because the strength of His humility is made perfect in weakness and foolishness.

God indeed revealed Himself and His Law on Mt. Sinai, but in terms of what was wrought and demonstrated by God, the cross eclipsed Sinai in its depth and significance. Yet, this act of God did not take place on a mountain top; it was not preceded by peals of lightning or wreaths of fire and smoke. The whole drama was enacted close to a garbage dump, outside the city, in a place where criminals were executed, by the act of nailing a naked Man to crossed pieces of wood, and thence suffering the agony of a cruel death. It is a statement about God that is infinitely more profound than the revelation of God that came at Sinai.

A crucified Messiah is a scandal to the world, and if the magnitude of that seeming contradiction has been lost to us, it is an unhappy statement of our own distance from God. God *intended* that the cross be a scandal; He intended it to contradict and confound. By understanding what underlies the crucifixion of Jesus and why it was God's explicit choice to end the life of His Son, the whole cosmic setting of the faith will be opened to us. Something was set in motion, not just in an historical moment of time in Palestine to a Jewish community of that era, but throughout all ages and into the ages to come.

Jesus suffered the worst of human indignities, for which reason mankind has the greatest difficulty conceiving of Him as being God. It is not in keeping with what they hold to be the dignity of God. The long-awaited Messiah was expected to come as a deliverer, not as a victim. Yet Paul says,

> For I determined to know nothing among you except Jesus Christ, and Him crucified. I was with you in weakness and in fear and in much trembling, and my message and my preaching were not in persuasive words of wisdom, but in demonstration of the Spirit and of power, so that your faith would not rest on the wisdom of men, but on the power of God.[96]

If we do not have that same determination—that is, to know nothing but Christ crucified—invariably other things will sneak in to subvert, to lessen, and eventually domesticate the radical content from our faith. Our faith will become just another conventional religious activity, bereft of any true power. It takes a determination to be single-eyed in presenting the scandal of the faith of God as He has depicted it on the cross. It required of Paul an act of self-denial, particularly for a man who was gifted with intellectual brilliance, to block out any other consideration. Paul was extremely careful about the way he conveyed the gospel, determining that the faith of his hearers should not be established upon any eloquence of man.

The astonishment of all that God has wrought in the scandal of the cross needs to apprehend us—that is, its amazing revelation must lay hold of us, it must reach through the fog and the filters of our inadequate understanding of God. If the message of salvation is not *this* message, then there is no basis for salvation. For Paul says that the gospel is foolishness to men, but to those who are saved it is the power of God. The scandal of the cross, which establishes the salvation of men, has

---

[96] 1 Corinthians 2:2-5

a power in it given by God. True preaching of the cross is always made in the manner of the cross—that is, in weakness, in foolishness, in trembling dependency. It requires a determination in the preacher *not* to allow any mode of expression that does not have its origin in God, nor any mode or style that does not reflect the qualities of foolishness in the eyes of the world, and a trembling dependency upon the Spirit of the Living God. An effectual bearing of the message of salvation to others is itself a re-enactment of the cross. The contrary is also true—where there is no effect, there is no cross. Having been saved by effectual preaching, and having come to faith by that preaching, we continue in that faith by being in Him who is made unto us wisdom from God, and righteousness, and sanctification, and redemption.[97]

> For the word of the cross is foolishness to those who are perishing, but to us who are being saved it is the power of God. For it is written, "I WILL DESTROY THE WISDOM OF THE WISE, AND The CLEVERNESS OF THE CLEVER I WILL SET ASIDE."

> Where is the wise man? Where is the scribe? Where is the debater of this age? Has not God made foolish the wisdom of the world? For since in the wisdom of God the world through its wisdom did not come to know God, God was well-pleased through the foolishness of the message preached to save those who believe.

> For indeed Jews ask for signs and Greeks search for wisdom; but we preach Christ crucified, to the Jews a stumbling block and to Gentiles foolishness, but to those who are the called, both Jews and Greeks, Christ the power of God and the

---

[97] See 1 Corinthians 1:30

wisdom of God. Because the foolishness of God is wiser than men, and the weakness of God is stronger than men.[98]

The world is drunk with power: electric power, atomic power, military power, and yes, personal power. People even look for their salvation in power terms. You hear phrases like, "powerful" men of God, "powerful" preachers. It sounds so spiritual, but how much of that is the celebration of man in our carnal motives? How about "weak" preachers? Consider Jesus who stood before His accusers, the Lamb who went silently to the slaughter. He demonstrated to them the power of the cross by His silence, humiliation, suffering, weakness, and finally His death. How many of us are actually ashamed and self-conscious about any form of weakness? Are we willing to risk appearing to be foolish in the eyes of the world and before one another, or do we prefer to save face, to come out "smelling like a rose" whenever we have that choice?

There needs to be power demonstrated by the church, but it needs to be the power of foolishness and weakness. It is the power of not succeeding on the basis of our own ability. It is the power that comes from a willingness to be weak in order to allow His life to be expressed. It is the power that comes in the fellowship of believers where our weaknesses are revealed, where we can allow our masks to come off so that God can show us what the truth of our real condition is. It is the power that comes from the willingness to be taken captive, to be restricted and to be constrained, through submission to God and to the brethren. It is the power that comes from self-denial—from the death of our self-life

---

[98] 1 Corinthians 1:18-25

To be restricted in a total dependency to live from the life of God is to taste humiliation. Only when we cease to draw from our own dependencies, however competent they may be, do we begin to see the transforming work of God through a life. To deny self is to determine not to trust in anything but the life of God and what He will give. When an individual or a fellowship lives in this kind of trust, it opens itself up to assault from the powers of darkness. The rulers, powers, and principalities in the kingdom of darkness hate anyone who takes seriously a willingness to walk in the way of foolishness and weakness. The church that has not this message will soon enough become emasculated, and the enemy rightly does not fear such a church; it cannot be an authentic church. It may continue in its religious forms, but it will not experience the vitality and power that comes with obedience to the foolishness of God.

> From the mouth of infants and nursing babes You have established strength because of Your adversaries, to make the enemy and the revengeful to cease.[99]

The wisdom of the enemy insists that for anyone to speak for God, they *must* be sophisticated and educated. They *must* have credentials and a degree. They *must* be a college or seminary graduate. However, the Scriptures say that God has chosen the infants and nursing babes, the foolish and weak things, to speak for Him. God has ordained strength out of that weakness because it contradicts the wisdom of the world. Silencing the enemy rests on our willingness to embrace weakness and foolishness, so that God might ordain strength through us *in our weakness*. A living faith is one of

---

[99] Psalm 8:2

dependence and trust; one that freely chooses, moment by moment, what God chooses. Faith calls for the forfeiture of any confidence or ability in ourselves to obtain what God has made available to us through the crucified and risen Christ. The two wisdoms are still in conflict.[100]

> For consider your calling, brethren, that there were not many wise according to the flesh, not many mighty, not many noble; but God has chosen the foolish things of the world to shame the wise, and God has chosen the weak things of the world to shame the things which are strong, and the base things of the world and the despised God has chosen, the things that are not, so that He may nullify the things that are, so that no man may boast before God.[101]

Weakness and foolishness are inherent in the faith. They are the key to the revelation of God's glory. Human pride, self-assurance and confidence in our ability to perform religious service for God will prevent us from seeing that glory. The spirit of the world has unquestionably affected us. The whole emphasis in church life today rests on the idea that we can "get the job done" as efficiently as the world. We use the world's techniques for building the kingdom of God. We can be just as charming, just as musical, just as organized, just as able. We can easily establish successful churches, movements, and organizations. In His mercy, the Lord will allow all these activities to fail—so as to show us that our humanistic hopes can never bring us to that true ground whereupon God can be Lord of all.

---

[100] See author's book: *Apostolic Foundations* for a fuller understanding of these wisdoms
[101] 1 Corinthians 1:26-29

Only a true work of God will compel the attention of the world. We need to be suspicious of anything that is outwardly impressive (in the world's eyes), anything that is well-funded (by the world's standards), anything that has ambitious building programs (according to the world's principles), anything with programs that crank out disciples like Henry Ford cranked out cars. If something seems to be working too well, and has been accomplished without the suffering of the cross, it is likely outside of the purposes of God. One of the reasons we show so little fruit or virtue in our lives is that so little is required of us, and we demand so little of ourselves. To compound the problem, those who lead us are fearful of requiring anything of us. An environment that challenges and confronts us ought to be more desired to counter the things that *we* establish for our own religious comfort and satisfaction. In other words, we need to embrace those things that are contrary to our self-serving desires. This does not mean we seek inconvenience and difficulty for their sake alone; we are not called to self-flagellation in any of its forms—we are, rather, enjoined to live in peace whenever it depends upon us. Yet we are called to embrace those elements of life, brought to us by God, that can sometimes blister our backs, blunt our foreheads, strip our wallets, and rip the very sinews from our hearts.

As long as we continue performing spiritual things in our own natural strength, our works will be dead rather than living and fruitful. True, life-giving fruit comes out of our willingness to be emptied—our willingness to die. Dying to self means making no demands; it means having no wall behind which one defends one's self. To be left defenseless is to be completely poured out, to remain foolish in the eyes of the world, and utterly weak in those things wherein the world considers important. And it is this weakness in the inmost place that God is seeking after.

It is not until we are saved and come into the fellowship of other believers that we really begin to learn and understand the dimensions of human depravity. The revelation of what we are in our humanity truly begins at that point. That is why the church, the *real* church, appears to be such a mess in the eyes of the world. Looking down from their well-organized, powerful, solidly financed congregational perspectives, they see in these true fellowships confusion, and contradiction and ugly revelations of the human condition. If we have not seen these unsightly travails in our church life and conduct, then where we are fellowshipping is not true church. If it "keeps the lid on" and "ensures that everyone appears prim and proper from all perspectives", if it is focused primarily upon activities which convey the semblance of "vibrant" church life, the "exulting" euphoria of meetings, songs, and "strong" preaching, then it is not sufficient to reveal what we are and what we all are together. Until we have come to recognize how wretched we are, how totally bankrupt and incapable we are of anything, and just how inclined we really are to live in the spirit of the world, then the grace of God is not available to us.

An authentic body of believers is one that is living the cruciform, cross-centered life. In this matrix, our individual sin becomes the larger issue of the fellowship with whom we are joined. We may *think* that it is a personal issue alone, but we are all affected by the sins of each individual. We do not have the strength to come out of our carnal tendencies and into the place of cross-centeredness except through the counsel, prayer, encouragement, witness and example of others around us who are of like faith.

Believers need to allow themselves to be placed into

situations and an environment where their humanistic, romantic ideas of the faith are shattered and destroyed. They must come to the place where they cannot go on. Ironically, it is at that point where life really begins, where God becomes God. That is where grace becomes grace. That is where He begins to unfold His will and His way; it is the place where He provides the power of His nature. But...He does so only after our own efforts fail to obtain it. Are we willing to be divested of human initiative and ability before we can be raised up into newness of life?

To demonstrate the "kingdom come" in our lives, we must first free ourselves from the petty kingdoms of man. We cannot leap over that necessity. The wisdom of the kingdoms of this world celebrates man's insistent confidence in his natural abilities and aptitudes. In the spiritual realm, man's reliance on his own competence ever seeks to want to know "how to" conduct services, "how to" perform ministry, "how to" implement programs and outreaches. Man's self-trust and continual searching after some formula or method is contrary to the wisdom of God. Those who forfeit any confidence in the natural man are those who also have a testimony to mankind powerful enough to save them from their foolish attempts to preserve themselves. Those who love not their lives are those who overcome the powers of this age.[102] This is the true faith. Have we said yes to *that* faith?

---

[102] See Revelation 12:11

CHAPTER 10

The Cross and Resurrection

God has made the supernatural event of resurrection the foundational condition for the salvation of mankind.

> That if you confess with your mouth Jesus as Lord, and believe in your heart that God raised Him from the dead, you will be saved.[103]

Here again, it is as if God has deliberately chosen something totally offensive to man. To the modern mind, the concept of resurrection seems impossible. It collides with human sensibility, logic, and rationality. Resurrection was difficult for the early disciples to consider. It was so contrary to their every reckoning that even though they witnessed that Jesus had been resurrected, they could not believe it."[104] We begin to get a sense that the root of resistance to the truth of resurrection is deeply planted in the human soul, even in those who should know better.

The resurrection of Jesus is the Father's approval and acceptance of the obedient death of Jesus, as a son,

---

[103] Romans 10:9
[104] See Luke 24:41

on the cross. God was validating Himself, showing His own approval of what He Himself established out of His own wisdom. He knew what was needed for the condition of mankind. This is why the resurrection of Jesus is more opposed by mankind than the crucifixion. In resurrecting Jesus from the dead, the Father was saying: "I am satisfied. I have received what You bore as the sinless Son of God becoming sin. You allowed the consequence and judgment for sin to fall upon You as altogether appropriate to My judgment. My righteous requirement has been fulfilled in Your death, and therefore You are raised. Your being raised out of death is the statement of My approval of the death that You suffered and the purposes for which You suffered it." God was approving Himself, validating His own wisdom. It was the careful, planned, predetermined act of the triune God.

God acts righteously and in keeping with His holy justice. He will act in mercy to forgive sin only on grounds that are righteous in His own sight, in keeping with His own righteousness. The death and resurrection of Jesus was that ground.

Resurrection can easily degenerate into a mere article of faith whereby it is affirmed as truth, but only as a credal truth, a concept that one subscribes to intellectually. It would be a situation akin to Paul's statement regarding a "form of godliness, although they have denied its power."[105] It is better that we do not have the form, than that we should have the form and deny the power that makes of the form the real thing.

---

[105] 2 Timothy 3:5

> Now if Christ is preached, that He has been raised from the dead, how do some among you say that there is no resurrection of the dead?[106]

Paul addresses a heresy that was taking root in the Corinthian church whereby some were denying that Christ had, indeed, risen from the dead. It was threatening the faith of the church at its heart. There is another form of this same denial amongst God's people today. We may not verbalize those exact words, "There is no resurrection from the dead," but the conduct of our lives testifies to that denial. The only way we can say that there is a resurrection is by the consistent demonstration of that power in our lives. Short of this resurrection reality and power, we will always seek to establish our own righteousness by our own works. Though we may give assent to the truth of the doctrine of resurrection, we are not living in the power of it, or in the righteousness of it. Therefore, we fall short of the glory of God.

The language we use betrays the extent of our knowledge of God. For example, we say, "If God will help me, then I will walk in the way." This implies that there are two independent entities: namely, God and me. Whether we say it or not, this is often our mentality. We do not see ourselves as dead men wholly thrust into a dependency upon the totality of His life. There is a world of difference between saying, "If God will help me," and Paul's statement, "For to me, to live is Christ."[107] Paul does not ask God to *help* him. Paul asks God to *be* him, to *be* his life, his speech, his conduct. Paul's whole sufficiency was Christ and knowing Him and the power of His resurrection.

---

[106] 1 Corinthians 15:12
[107] Philippians 1:21a

122

There is a totality about resurrection that needs to be understood and appropriated; it is exclusively and entirely *of* God. God will raise us into a union with Himself *if* we are convinced of the necessity for our own death to our natural self. As long as we feel that we can get by with our puny religious wisdom and understanding, we will fall short of His glory. Death to all confidence in the flesh is God's inexorably fixed law of life. Resurrection is only resurrection when it is life from death. God takes the sword and cuts right through anything that is predicated upon human progress and improvement. He offers as an alternative an *event*—the resurrection event. This "God-event" is stark, absolute, and totally dependent upon Him who gives it, when He will give it.

Unregenerate mankind prefers evolutionary processes, gradual changes and the comforting assuagement of slow, dawning sequences of realization. Resurrection negates all that in favor of God's exclusive power to quicken to life in the moment of His choosing. Process implies the involvement of man through his ever-developing understanding; in its essence it defers to and depends upon man. Resurrection absolutely and utterly defers to and depends upon God, leaving no room for man at all.

In our human effort, we may attain to certain degrees of very impressive ethical conduct. Our lives can never be a glory, however, because our whole framework of life is on the human side of a great abyss. And if it is on the human side of the abyss, it does not matter whether our deeds are evil or seemingly good, they both come from our natural man. We inhabit a "body of death," and that is why Paul cried out, "Who will set me free from the body of this death? Thanks be to God through Jesus Christ our Lord!"[108] To believe in Christ is to believe for His resurrection. This is a far cry from our humanistic tendency that hopes for progressive change, which is not hoping in the true hope; and that is why we desperately look around for some alternative to the ever-present death in our fellowships. We embrace any kind of innovation in an attempt to find an answer to our woes, not knowing that we are rooted on the human side of the abyss. We say, "Well, maybe power evangelism will be the key; maybe the church growth movement is the answer; maybe a series of programs is what we need; maybe the prosperity message; maybe the new apostolic and prophetic movement; maybe we can laugh ourselves into revival; maybe if we made our churches more relevant to today's culture."

Many different kinds of "faith" abound in Christendom. Many quote scriptures and seek to hold God to His word for His promises. To grow in that kind of confidence is not true faith. Many of us will need to put away that kind of false faith in order to come into the faith of the Son of God. It will require a wrenching to let go of something in which we have placed our confidence, security, and identity. There is a no-man's land of nothingness between the end of our humanly-contrived "faith" and the beginning of the faith of God. We bring our human substitute to death in bringing it to the cross. We abandon it as much as if it were sin. We look upon our own meager attempt at faith with the same kind of loathing and detesting as if it were sin. For true faith to come, we need to rid ourselves of that lesser thing. Death at the cross is the entry into the realm of divine faith.

---

[108] Romans 7:24b-25a

Dead, lifeless, innocuous fellowships proliferate everywhere. The preaching is dull and lacking in anointing, lacking in true spiritual power to bring about a difference in the lives of the ones who hear the preaching. The worship is either listless or sensual. It is a drag to go through the meeting; you almost dread for Sunday to come again. The fellowship is shallow; the service is relentlessly predictable; week after week the same thing. You have prayed for the preacher, the pastor, but nothing changes. To be blunt, it is an absolute suffering to be there. It is so tempting to seek another fellowship. Will you remain and abide in a place of death until the resurrection comes? Can there ever be an authentic expression of fellowship without first the willingness to taste death on behalf of that fellowship?

Unless we are willing to bear the ordinary and undistinguished days, we can forget about the glorious ones. It is always *His* good pleasure and *His* will. Yesterday's mountaintop experience served His purpose, but today's time in the dry, dusty valley serves His purpose equally as profoundly. Are we willing to be cast upon God for His life? Unless life had come to Jesus while He was in the tomb, He would have remained in that death. He relinquished His life unto death. He had no power or influence in what would happen from that point. He trusted in God in a faith unto death, thereby defining faith in its deepest and truest sense.

A.W. Tozer wrote, "We must do something about the cross, and one of two things only we can do: flee it or die upon it."[109] There is nothing in between. We cannot partially commit some aspect of our life and keep

---

[109] A.W.Tozer: *The Cross is a Radical Thing*

the rest. The cross is the place of death. We cannot keep alive our virtues, our gifts, our theological intellect, or other admirable aspects about our natural life. That is where death becomes death for us, but that is exactly what Jesus gave up as the Son of Man. Tozer adds that the cross will cut into our lives where it hurts most, sparing neither us nor our carefully cultivated reputations. It will defeat us and bring our selfish lives to an end. Only then shall we rise in fullness of life to establish a pattern of living wholly new and free, and full of good works. But the church that compromises the message of the cross will perish.[110]

To live outside the resurrection condemns us to a deformed state of living. To willfully continue to function in our own human strength and religious abilities while knowing that there needs to be a crucifixion and a death to that strength and those abilities for true life to flow forth, is a slap in the face toward God. To serve God outside of His life is a complete disregard for the enormous act that God has performed in the crucifixion of Jesus and the raising of Him from the dead. To be satisfied with resurrection as a doctrine without living from that provision is to despise the grace of God.

Ironically, when that false basis is challenged, a severity of retaliation and opposition are often the very testimony that two different modes of life are in collision. The natural life can be skillful, knowledgeable, competent, and powerful. But when that natural life is threatened by the resurrection life, it will seek to extinguish the one through whom that life is expressed. When we understand that dynamic, we will understand why Christ was crucified; He was a threat to

---

[110] Ibid.

an entire religious mode of being, an entire system that encouraged men to act out of their own life and establish their own righteousness. The final outworking of that threat was to crucify the One who offered the grace of the righteousness of God.

> "Men of Israel, listen to these words: Jesus the Nazarene, a man attested to you by God with miracles and wonders and signs which God performed through Him in your midst, just as you yourselves also know—this Man, delivered over by the predetermined plan and foreknowledge of God, you nailed to a cross by the hands of godless men and put Him to death."[111]

Peter's sermon reveals the sovereign will of God in predetermining the crucifixion of Jesus. It does not, because of that, absolve men of their culpability and responsibility as participants in that death. Peter's indictment of their involvement and guilt is the basis for which he calls them to repentance. If they were not responsible, there is no basis for appealing to them to "repent, and...be baptized."[112] God's sovereignty predetermines, yet men act out of their own freewill. Therefore, we can confront every man as a sinner, guilty not only in his own sin, but equally in *this* sin. We would all have done the same thing were we there, and therefore we are just as responsible as those who participated in the actual event.

To refuse to live in the grace and power of God's life reveals that we are moral cowards, having a greater security and confidence in living from ourselves than in trusting the life of God. We are unwilling to bring to death our own self-dependence because we prefer to

---

[111] Acts 2:22-23
[112] Acts 2:38a

function from that place. We are unwilling to let go and trust the life of God that He might be glorified.

The Lord is waiting for us to give up the ghost and say, "Lord, we have tried everything to live the Christian life, but we have been flaying a dead horse." God waits for that acknowledgment. But how many of us are incorporating into our church life certain provisions and safeguards so that we will never become totally desperate, never become a total failure?

How do we know if we are living out of His resurrection life or out of our own strength? We can know by how we respond when the truth of our spirituality is questioned. If our reaction is angry, defensive, or self-justifying, if we protest too much, if we always want to have the last word, one final say in a matter, we are likely evidencing a life lived outside of His. On the other hand, the willingness to put aside ourselves, our hopes, our interests, our reputation, our ambitions, our self-esteem, our confidence in order to bear what comes to us in foolishness and weakness is likely the fruit of a life lived in God.

Paul could say, "O DEATH, WHERE IS YOUR VICTORY? O DEATH, WHERE IS YOUR STING?"[113] The fear of death, which has terrified mankind since time immemorial, is broken. Once you come out of the fear of death, what fear shall touch you? Of what shall you then be afraid? You are in another realm; you are in the resurrection; you are no longer a squealing animal wanting to be vindicated.

> Jesus said to them, "The sons of this age marry
> and are given in marriage, but those who are
> considered worthy to attain to that age and the
> resurrection from the dead, neither marry nor are

---

[113] 1 Corinthians 15:55

given in marriage; for they cannot even die anymore, because they are like angels, and are sons of God, beings sons of the resurrection."[114]

Though Jesus is referring to a future time when marriage does not occur, the sons and daughters of the resurrection attain to that blessed state in this life. If they do marry here on earth in this age, they do not do so on any natural basis or outward looks. God has joined them; that is the only reason. Even in that joining, their marriage is not like other marriages. Though married, they live as purposefully in undistracted devotion to the Lord as those who are not married.[115] They do not ignore their spouses, but they also do not look upon them with adoring fascination and singular attention as if there were no higher purpose for their being. They prefigure another kind of relationship that is totally at odds with a world that predicates marriage on the basis of self-interest and self-gratification.

The church can only fulfill its mandate to a dying world on the basis of resurrection. Well-meaning intentions and any other basis by which we are presently motivated will end in frustration and defeat. To be in the resurrection *now* is to be ushered into a remarkable place; we will find that everything in our daily lives will be charged with a deepened, heightened significance.

Have you chosen what God has chosen? The crucifixion of Jesus is the statement of God's choice, the statement of God's wisdom. It has been validated and verified by raising the Crucified One from the dead. God honored His own choice by validating that death in resurrection, and He will validate ours in resurrection

---

[114] Luke 20:34-36
[115] 1 Corinthians 7:29, 35

when we choose death. It is voluntary. Jesus was not dragged kicking to the cross: "I lay My life down."[116] And so must we also. Far better that we should know this, and choose this now, than think that we will be able to make a decision of this kind later in life when the world and its ways, its fortunes, and what we have acquired in it will make such a choice virtually impossible. Choose ye now, this day.

---

[116] John 10:18

PRAYER

Lord, You were marred more than any man. There was nothing left of any beauty that we should desire You. You were smitten of God. The abuse that was inflicted upon Your naked body should never have come upon a holy Son. You suffered the abandonment of Your Father. You were the ultimate sin offering.

We have all transgressed. We are all guilty of going our own way, unwilling to acknowledge the truth of our condition. May we not add in any way to what You have already borne by our own light regard of the truth of our condition. May we see and understand the evil that Your Father's holy name needed to requite at Your expense, for which You were willing. You did not let that cup pass. We ask Your forgiveness for our own failure and the failure of the church to uphold the truth of Your great act, which is at the heart of all reality.

Help us with a true revelation of Your willingness to be wounded for *our* transgressions and bruised for *our* iniquities. Put something deep into our inner man that will temper every aspect of our lives. Our whole demeanor has got to be affected by this epochal, once-and-for-all event. Save us from conducting cheap Sunday services for the benefit of men, their pleasure, and self-esteem.

Your suffering unto death was pleasing to the Father, or You would not have been resurrected. He raised You out of a sealed cave guarded by armed Roman soldiers lest someone steal Your body. Despite all that, You were raised from death as the statement of the Father's approval of the efficacy of that sacrifice. Give us a hatred of iniquity when we see what was required to expiate it, that we would not even dare to allow the appearance of it, that we would love righteousness, that we would take Your admonition to be holy as You are holy.

Help the church find its way back to the cross. Redeem our clumsy and inadequate effort to see what has been made of the extraordinary sacrifice of Your Son. Forgive us for making the cross an article to dangle from our neck, or a piece of church architecture and decoration.

May we be jealous for the truth of the cross, and be willing for the implications of it. Give us a willingness to bear its inconvenience, and even to suffer for it. Give us a jealousy for the truth that makes us to examine our own heart and our own condition. We ask that You touch us in the deeps, and show us where we ourselves have not been jealous to maintain the truth. Show us where we ourselves are evasive, where we have shrunk from the implications of the cross for ourselves, where we have not identified with the suffering Christ, not willing ourselves to suffer.

We will not give up till we have examined your cross to *Your* complete satisfaction. May You hear from us a word of surrender, a willingness to bear the cross, and in that, to come into a true union with You. Bring these words constantly to our recall. Thank you for Your great provision, and receive our gratitude. Amen.

OTHER BOOKS
by Art Katz

REALITY: THE HOPE OF GLORY
The four messages in this book are a powerful inspiration to those who will not settle for less than the true meaning of life as a disciple of Christ.
Paperback, 156 pages.

THE SPIRIT OF TRUTH
Into this age of religious pretension, exaggeration and deception, Art brings a deep, incisive probing into the nature of truth. Every lover and guardian of truth will find this an insightful and demanding book.
Paperback, 101 pages.

BEN ISRAEL – ODYSSEY OF A MODERN JEW
Written as a literal journal, Art recounts his experience as an atheist and former Marxist being apprehended by a God whom he was not seeking. The message of this book has been powerfully used to bring other of Art's Jewish kinsmen to the faith of their fathers.
Paperback, 149 pages.

TRUE FELLOWSHIP – *Church as Community*
When God called us to establish a Christian community, I knew that it was a call to the cross, to humiliation and suffering. We were going to be living closely and intensively with other believers on a daily basis in which our defects, our shortcomings and our failures would be revealed. Out of the agonies and the joys, we gave opportunity for a reality to come forth that can best be described as "true fellowship." Paperback, 146 pages.

THE ANATOMY OF DECEPTION
In a dark and seductive age, and one that is increasingly abounding in deception and lying signs, the ability to discern between the false and the true is of paramount importance. Paperback, 60 pages.

THE PROPHETIC CALL – *True and False Prophets*
If we cannot distinguish between the prophets that are true and those that are false, it is a statement that we are unable to distinguish between the God who is true and the god who is false. Art seeks to identify the essential elements of what makes a prophet true, and by that, he gives a corresponding glimpse into the truth of God as He in fact is. Paperback, 110 pages.

THE HOLOCAUST: WHERE WAS GOD?
– An inquiry into the biblical roots of tragedy.
In a daring hypothesis, the author turns to the ancient Hebrew scriptures as the key of interpretation to one of the most catastrophic events of modern times: the Jewish Holocaust of World War II. In this examination of that ultimate tragedy, the issue of God *as God* is brought courageously to the forefront of our modern consideration as few books have attempted to do. Paperback, 91 pages.

WHAT A JEW DOES WITH JESUS
Despite the apparent contradiction, the author pleads with his Jewish kinsmen to take into their deepest consideration the truth that biblical Judaism is determined solely by what we do with Jesus of Nazareth. Paperback, 128 pages.

THE TEMPTATIONS OF CHRIST
– *A Call to Sonship and Maturity*
The scriptures indicate that Jesus was led into the wilderness in the *fullness* of the Spirit, but came out of that testing place in the *power* of the Spirit. The author examines the necessary progression in our Christian lives without which we will never be able to convey the knowledge of the risen Christ. Paperback, 56 pages.

DACHAU – A SILENT WITNESS
Art takes up the subject of the silence of God during one of the darkest moments of Jewish calamity, and insists that the seeming absence of God, when rightly understood, is a key to the true knowledge of His reality and presence. Booklet, 35 pages.

APOSTOLIC FOUNDATIONS
In his penetrating manner, Art shows that a church with apostolic foundations is a body of people whose central impulse is a radical and total jealousy for the glory of God. It was so at the church's inception, and needs to be so at its conclusion. Paperback, 235 pages.